# The Wild Side of Alaska

Donna Morang

ISBN-13: 978-1490390833

ISBN-10: 1490390839

For Cathy Speight

An amazing lady who asks nothing, and gives it all.

# *Acknowledgments*

I am grateful to my first readers:

Mr. John Howard, who was familiar with hunting, and living in Alaska kept me thinking, and rewriting those messy pages.

Ms. Elena Hiatt Houlihan, who drew many red lines through the chapters she critiqued, and pushed me forward to continue with my memoir.

Thankfully, I found David VanDyke, who carefully polished my manuscript, and deleted numerous commas (because I am known as the queen of commas) David also made me feel proud of what I had written, and was a joy to work with.

I am beholden to Cathy Speight for her never-ending support, and endless editing, I owe her dozens and dozens of roses. She is the best friend anyone could have, and I have never met her, yet she has read, edited, read, and again edited my manuscript because she is simply that dedicated to making The Wild Side of Alaska, look pretty.

Eternal thanks to my artists and designers, Nidia Verónica Galindo Aldape, and Cuauhtli Rivera Ramos for once again creating an amazing cover, and those spectacular interior sketches.

Last but not least I want to thank my readers. You are the most important, without you, there would be no need to write.

## CHAPTER 1
# MONTANA TO CANADA

Swiping my older brother's pellet gun at the age of six was the beginning of my love of pulling the trigger and of the excitement of seeing where I had hit the target. The first time I picked up that coveted gun, I didn't stop firing until the little tin box holding the pellets was almost empty. Then my brother walked around the corner and discovered me lying on our front lawn shooting into our white picket fence.

He wasn't upset with me for using his gun but instead offered advice. "Hey, Sis, Mom's going to kill you for shooting the fence full of holes. Go shoot at some tin cans, for Pete's sake. If I were you, I'd get out of here before she sees all those fresh holes." His recommendation of shooting at cans and moving farther away from our mother's view probably saved me from a well-deserved spanking. He generously gave me his old pellet gun that day, so I no longer had to steal it.

I shot hundreds of pellets at those cans lined up on the river bank, but for several months there were more misses than hits. I slowly improved my aim, and a couple of years later, my brother and I held daily shooting contests. We would put up targets at varying distances, and I did well at close range, but at long range my little gun didn't have enough power to hit the bull's-eye, so he would be the daily winner. I didn't think it was fair because he had a scope and a .22, while I still only had a pellet gun. I bet him that if I could use his .22 for a week, I could out-shoot him. If I won, I got his .22. If I lost, I would owe him twenty dollars.

With that bet won, I moved up to a bigger gun. With my new .22 in hand, I would hunt gophers all day long. My father was quite happy with my shooting skills, as the varmints were abundant and digging fresh holes in our pastures. My mother was less thrilled with my shooting, as she would have much preferred me to take dancing lessons.

The year I turned ten, my uncle loaned me his .25-20 Winchester lever-action rifle for my first deer hunt. I was excited to be included in this male-only trip, but my father quickly squelched that feeling. He told me I had to stay inside the truck because there were too many people hunting that day, and it was too dangerous. Broken-hearted and quite angry, I sat in the cab of the truck on the day I thought would be the most exciting of my life. I ate my lunch, took a nap, and sat staring out the window of that stupid truck for what seemed like hours. I imagined deer hiding behind every blade of grass that moved, and thoughts of sneaking up to a huge buck filled my head.

As I sat looking and dreaming, a huge mule deer buck slowly walked out of the trees and right up to where I was. I slowly rolled the window down, stuck a shell in my gun, and fired, just as I would have done if it were a tin can. That was the first time I had ever shot anything other than small varmints, and this beautiful deer lay dead not ten feet from the truck.

Hearing a shot from near the truck, my father and uncle came running. I don't know who was more surprised—them or me—but I know they were stunned. I think they thought just taking me along was a way to placate me, and I thought that was how hunting worked: if you saw a good-sized buck, you shot it, took it home, and enjoyed many delicious meals.

I had more lessons to learn, and the first one that day was how to field-dress a deer. My father handed me his pocket knife and carefully explained how to hold the knife and where to enter the deer's hide. Because it was a buck, he explained, it was a little different from dressing a doe. He guided my hand and said, "Now, this is the tricky part, so go slow, relax, and let my hand guide yours."

After what seemed like two hours of hard work, my deer was gutted and ready to be hung in the meat house. There it would hang for a week of aging and becoming more tender and better-tasting. When it was properly aged, my father taught me how to skin the hide away leaving only the delicious meat. He taught me the fine art of cutting it into chops and roasts, wrapping and marking each package with 'Donna's deer.' A few special cuts were cooled for a day in the refrigerator. Being the great cook he was, he taught me how to fry a deer chop perfectly, using lots of butter to give it added flavor. I'm quite sure my deer's tenderloin that day was the best meat I had ever tasted.

Throughout my early years of hunting, I successfully took several deer with that gun, but I learned early on I had to be darned close to the animal before taking a shot with the .25-20, or I would end up with a wounded animal. After a discussion with my Uncle Tige, we decided it was a much better idea for me to use his 250-3000 Savage if I wanted to keep hunting.

That rifle became my favorite until later in life when I purchased my very own gun. Saving my money, I bought a Montana Centennial 6mm bolt action because it was a caliber that impressed me, but it was also so beautiful, I had to own one. It was the most elegant gun I had ever seen, with a one-hundred-year Montana territory centennial coin inlaid into a nutmeg laminated stock. I paid $125 at that time and used it throughout Montana for deer, antelope, and black bear.

That same gun today trades for a thousand dollars, and mine is still in mint condition. Even though I used it for years, being my pride and joy, I was always protective of it. Sorry to say, but that .25-20 was the last gun I owned with open sights, and I can no longer hit the broad side of a barn without a scope on any gun. I still cherish that little pellet gun and fondly remember the day I stole it from my brother, Joe, but I had to move on to bigger and better rifles.

I'm quite sure that growing up on a ranch in Montana with two brothers and mainly boys to play with led to my love of hunting and fishing, rather than doing girly things like playing with dolls. Being from Two Dot, Montana, it was a time without television, and kids were required to entertain themselves, so my choices were to shoot, fish, or go camping with my cousin.

I often did all three together with my cousin. Di and I would gather our tent, pots and pans, jump into our jeep, and camp alongside the river, where we would catch fish, shoot a few tin cans, and smoke cigarettes we stole from my father. We sometimes even smoked the horrid driftwood found at the river's edge. It was a time to explore and grow to be adventuresome women. It may have been the birth of our own personal women's movement. We were free to hunt, fish, ride horses, and conquer the world. Even through high school, when girls wanted to be cheerleaders or prom queens, I just wanted to shoot, fish, camp, and win the big-buck contest held annually in our local area.

This contest was a county-wide event, held from the opening to the closing day of the hunting season, sponsored by the local sporting-goods store. The year I was eleven—and too young to enter the contest—I shot a six-point Mulley (Western count, not Eastern) with a huge antler span. It was an incredible day of hunting. The tough old mountain deer had been pushed out of the Crazy Mountains by a winter storm, and we found them down in the river bottoms. It seemed that beside every cottonwood tree there hid a massive mule deer buck.

My father, uncle, two brothers, and I each scored a big one that day; however, mine measured the largest. Being the scoundrel he was, my uncle entered my deer into the contest in his name. Yes, Uncle Tige was the winner that year, and he thought it was darn good fun that a little girl had beaten all the other hunters. That was as close as I came to winning the big-buck contest in Wheatland County.

It was a natural evolution for me to date boys who hunted and fished. I found one, dated him through high school, and then married him. Together Hub and I spent years hunting or fishing in Montana, but our biggest dream was to live in Alaska. We talked about it day and night. We read everything in the local library and bought every magazine that had anything pertaining to Alaska. Hub applied for every teaching job listed in the state of Alaska and made calls to several school districts to check on openings in his field of science or counseling. Our dreams were filled with this exciting last frontier, where hunting and fishing were reported to be the biggest and the best in North America. Then one day it happened!

The phone rang, and it was the director of the North Star Borough School District. I was so excited, I almost dropped the phone. Yelling like an idiot, I screamed at Hub to hurry. I'm certain the director was questioning what kind of person he had hired. At least Hub remained calm while he spoke to him. As soon as the phone was down, we were screaming, laughing, hugging, and dancing in circles. Hub had done it! He had been selected for one of the teaching jobs. We were moving to Fairbanks, Alaska.

We immediately started calling friends and family to celebrate our victory. Then we went shopping for everything we thought we would need and couldn't buy in Alaska. My father bought Hub and me new fishing rods, and I became the proud owner of a .350 Remington Winchester Magnum, recommended as the ultimate big gun for Alaskan hunting. The final purchase was the crème de la crème of all Alaska travel books: *The Milepost*.

By the time we left for our trip, this book was coffee-stained, dog-eared, and considerably worn. It was highlighted for all the essential roadside services, camping grounds, even where to get the best apple pie or a good night's lodging. We almost felt like we had already traveled the predicted fifteen hundred miles of gravel road. We were prepared and excited to fulfill our dreams of heading north.

Then the reality of leaving home hit me. I wouldn't be able to drop by and see my friends or family for a long, long time. This was something I hadn't thought about in my dreams of Alaska. As we drove way from my home in Two Dot, Montana, I saw my father standing in the big picture window of our kitchen. He gave a brief goodbye wave, and then I saw him wipe his eyes.

My father was a tough Montana cowboy, who didn't cry over anything. He had tried to teach me to be the same, yet there he was, crying. His tears flattened my excitement like a slap in the face. I too started to cry, so I stopped looking at him, but then all I could see were the rugged Crazy Mountains and the deep cut of Big Elk Canyon. These mountains were the sentinels of my life in Montana, their shapes and colors rimming my view for twenty-four years. It shocked me that I could leave behind my home and my family with just a wave of the hand, and my eyes were leaking like a sieve. Every time I stopped crying, we made another stop to say goodbye to friends, and the tears would start again. I think that first day, Hub drove as fast and furiously as the law allowed just so he wouldn't have to look at my tear-stained face or listen to my blubbering. Within three or four hours, we were out of Montana and crossing into Canada.

OUR ADVENTURE HAD BEGUN.

CHAPTER 2

# OH CANADA

When we entered Canada, with our camper shell filled with everything we owned, the border guard asked if we had any guns. "Yes, sir, we do, but we'll have to unload a lot of things before we can show them to you." He politely directed us to pull over to a little side stand, where we had to fill out papers in triplicate and plug the barrel of each gun and seal them.

There were instructions on to how to care for our guns at the stand. It was a self-service at best, and it seemed like they trusted us to do as instructed. We needed to use a hand-held machine that inserted a plastic plug into the barrel, and then we secured it into a plastic bag with a Canadian-stamped metal seal.

When we had this strange job completed and the papers filled out, we crossed the road back to customs, and another Royal Canadian Mounted Police officer came to check on the process. He stressed how important this was because when we left Canada, the RCMP would check our guns again to make sure each one registered was still sealed and hadn't been used in Canada.

Passports weren't required at that time, but because we were transporting weapons, the paperwork confirmed who we were, how many guns we had, what caliber they were, and the serial number of each. This gave us a legal license to transport our weapons inside Canada for sixty days. Speaking with the RCMP in their impressive uniforms, entering a foreign country, and sealing our weapons were pretty exciting events for two young people just starting their adventure in Alaska.

With all our stops and starts, we didn't get far that first day. By the end of the second, I was tired of seeing the flatlands of Montana and the same in Alberta. It seemed the wheat fields would never end. However, there were always majestic mountains in the background, with white snowcaps peaking towards the heavens, but the highway led us through nothing but flat land and not such picturesque country.

After traveling about a thousand miles, we finally arrived in Dawson Creek, British Colombia, and mile zero of the Alcan Highway. I don't recall if Dawson Creek was overly spectacular or not; I was just so excited to be there. It might have looked better to my eyes than in reality. I think I took a dozen pictures of the sign announcing 'Milepost 0 of the Alcan Highway.' It was the beginning of a long-planned adventure, which had become a reality.

Leaving lovely-dream-come-true Dawson, we hoped to get to Laird Hot Spring by late afternoon. This was going to be our first night not sleeping in a motel. We had packed a roll-away bed at the back of our camper, specifically for camping out along the way, and that was our plan for the night.

Arriving at Laird in the late afternoon, we set up our camp and took a warm dip in the primitive Laird Hot Spring. This was just a small area someone had dug out and cleared around the hot springs. This little spot was wonderful with super-hot water flowing in one spot and icy cold at the other end. I think it's now much more elegant and touristy than back in 1967. It made a delightful break, but lots of mosquitoes buzzed around our heads. We rolled out our bed, lit some charcoal, and cooked a steak.

We were quite happy with the five hundred miles we had driven that day and climbed into bed about the time the sun was going down. Once it had gone down, it sounded as if a small airplane was circling overhead, but I knew it was just the same swarm of mosquitoes, and they and all their cousins had come to drink our blood.

It wasn't long before Hub curled up in the cab of the truck. I buried my head under the covers, plugged my ears, and yelled for the mosquito spray. It was a long and nasty night, to say the least. If you've never been to northern British Canada or Alaska, you don't know what a mosquito really looks like. These critters are so big and numerous, they could carry a small child away. Okay, I'm stretching things a tiny bit, but the truth is, it was the last time we rolled that bed out of our camper for the duration of the trip, neither of us being brave enough to face the swarming blood-suckers again.

After our nasty night with such poor sleep, we made plans to drive to Whitehorse, Yukon Territory. It would only be four hundred miles and not the usual five hundred we had planned to do each day. Pulling into Whitehorse at the edge of town for gas, as the attendant filled our tank, he advised us, "You'd better keep on going because there isn't a hotel room open tonight or even tomorrow night." Not believing him, we stopped at two hotel/motels and were told the same: no rooms in the whole town. It was getting later than we liked to travel, but not having a choice we kept going. We stopped at anywhere that resembled suitable lodging for a night. An hour or so later, we pulled into a sketchy-looking place that had a sign hanging on a tree saying 'Vacancy.' Yes, they had a room, and we took it sight unseen.

This turned out to be the nastiest place I've ever stayed in. The beds were so dirty, Hub got his sleeping bag out rather than climb into the sheets, and I just shook my head in disgust. I couldn't bring myself to even look at the filthy bathroom. I chose the cab of the pickup for the night, and I used the spot behind the trees rather than that toilet. Since that night, I've traveled to many third-world countries, and that was the filthiest place I've ever seen, and it wasn't cheap.

I don't know if it was the bedbugs that woke Hub early or the stench, but we got out of there bright and early that morning. All we saw were just more large trees along the roadway, blocking out anything scenic, with only a glimpse of beauty now and then and more dusty gravel roads. Rocks flying, dirt and dust filling the pickup cab, and our noses seemed to be the law of the Alcan Highway. Every so often we would stop at a lake or a river crossing and try a little fishing, but it sure wasn't anything special, as we were only in places where others before us had stopped to try their luck.

My job as co-pilot and milepost reader was as important as Hub's driving. Hitting one of the giant chuckholes could have meant a broken axle, and believe me, there were thousands to miss. It was slow-driving most of the time, with me yelling to him, "Hole on the right, one on the left." Then, if we missed the gas station the milepost recommended as a designated fill-up, we either ran out of fuel or had to go back because there were no more gas stations for over one hundred miles. If we didn't stop at 'The Shack' for breakfast, it was a long haul until the next roadhouse for lunch.

We made a few errors along the way. Occasionally finding a roadhouse closed for an unknown reason, we would have to eat a can of tuna or a day-old sandwich on the never-ending roadside.

No matter what else changed, the Milepost guide book was always accurate with the signs 'WARNING: potholes and rough road.' Two Dot, Montana, to Fairbanks, Alaska, was two thousand three hundred miles of not great roads. In 1967, even the roads in Montana were narrow and many still unpaved, but after about fifteen hundred miles of the Alcan's potholes, frost heaves, and dusty gravel roads, I felt like a 'sourdough' (Alaskan old-timer) already.

With four hundred more miles behind us, we arrived in Haines Junction, milepost 1016 of the Alcan Highway. Haines was a cute little spot on the road with one hotel and a couple of restaurants, but the brilliant blue sky and the mountains in the background were spectacular. It was pure eye candy to finally see something other than trees, trees, and more trees lining the highway. I was just happy to sit at the edge of Lake Kluane, looking at huge glaciers on the mountain peaks close by and hillsides filled with flowers. This was how I had envisioned our trip up the Alcan would be once we left the wheat fields of Alberta and Montana behind. I had never expected miles and miles of seeing nothing but trees.

This lovely picturesque area reminded me of the summer Hub and I manned a lookout in the Little Belt Mountains of Montana, and it was equally stunning. We had been hired by the Forest Service to watch for forest fires in the Little Belts and the Helena National Forest. Our tiny ten-by-ten glass house in the sky, sitting fifty feet from the ground was known as a fire lookout station. The elevation of the mountain was already at seven thousand four hundred feet and adding the fifty feet into the air, we claimed a view of unbelievable beauty. At that altitude, climbing and carrying buckets of water up four flights of stairs daily, I felt like a mountain goat or as if I were training for the Olympics. It was a unique experience, to say the least.

The first day, the head U.S. forest ranger from our district deposited us at Monument Lookout. Then he and Hub went to the river to fetch our weekly water supply, leaving me alone to man the lookout.

Minutes after their departure, a horrific lightning storm surrounded the structure. Being a novice, fresh from firefighting school and only slightly trained on this thing they called an azimuth compass, where I was supposed to chart each lightning strike, I prepared to do battle. Nervously, I jumped up onto the stool, pulled it up to this azimuth thing, grabbed a pencil, and marked every lightning strike on the map, just as I had been trained in firefighting school. I did remember what they told us in class: *Do not touch anything metal, sit on a wooden stool with insulators, and move the compass with a wooden pencil, not your fingers.* What else did they tell us? I forgot because then I was too busy marking strikes on my map.

With each strike I whirled the azimuth compass, marking each one on the map. I marked over a hundred strikes, with many more being just the cloud-to-cloud types and not recordable. They lit up the sky around my scared little body for at least thirty minutes. With sweat pouring off my nose, I was sure one of those strikes would find that wetness and zap me dead, but this was my job, so I kept marking the strikes. When the men returned, the big honcho from the forest service asked, "How many strikes did you map?"

Nervously, I replied, "I think there were over a hundred hits."

He laughed and told me, "We'll keep you around if you don't quit today. Damn, but that was one of the worst storms I've ever seen up here."

"It really was exciting, but what will happen if I didn't mark every hit?"

Again he gave a hearty laugh and replied, "Well, if you missed any, you'll know when you see smoke. From the looks of all those strikes, they were so close to your new home, the only thing you need to worry about is the mountain you're sitting on will be on fire—or more likely, the lookout will burn down."

So began our summer at Monument Lookout. There ceased to be concerns of fire in our district because it rained most of the summer, and we had snow by the middle of August. Our daily life soon consisted of many hands of cribbage or pinochle and going up and down the four flights of stairs to visit the outhouse instead of watching for fires.

Because of the diminished danger of fire, we closed the wooden shutters on our glass house and were transferred to a cabin near to the main office. This is where we spent the end of summer and where we were placed on campground detail, advising campers to clean up after themselves and check to see if they had a shovel, bucket, and an axe, as was required for camping in the mountains. It wasn't my favorite part of the summer. I much preferred the strange life in our glass house overlooking the majestic Belt Mountains that reminded me of this Canadian area.

With Haines in our rearview mirror, we were eager to leave the Yukon Territory to enter Alaska at Tok Junction. We had our guns ready for inspection and all the paperwork we had previously filled out back in Sweetgrass, Montana, crossing into Canada. At customs, the RCMP looked over our papers and then checked our guns. Everything was in order, and we departed Canada. Even back in 1967, there stood a much-desired wooden sign that said, 'Welcome to Alaska—The Last Frontier.' I believe we took a dozen pictures of each of us at that sign. Alaska: the land we had dreamed about for several years—and there we were.

The trip to Fairbanks on that day was filled with excitement with both of us often talking at the same time. We were like two little kids. We found a Fairbanks radio station to listen to, but with all our chitchat, neither of us heard much. When we passed through the town of North Pole—yes, it really is a little town a few miles outside Fairbanks—I thought it had to be the sweetest place on earth. It looked like Santa truly must have lived there.

I don't think we had eaten anything that morning, with all the hurry to get to Fairbanks, and when we pulled into an A&W on the edge of town, we both ordered hamburgers and fries. My excitement ended when we got the bill; these hamburgers were three dollars each, six times the normal price. Oh my god. We were used to paying fifty cents for a burger, not three dollars. All I hoped for was that we had enough money to make it until Hub started teaching on September 1.

We were lucky to have a place to stay until we found our own spot. Hub had an aunt who taught in Fairbanks, and because she was on vacation, she graciously loaned us her apartment in the Northward Building. Thinking we wouldn't be eating at the A&W very often, I went to Safeway to get groceries. That was the next big shock: a loaf of bread was thirty-five cents in Montana, and there, it was one dollar. I picked up a rather sad head of lettuce, and at the check-out stand, I decided we wouldn't be having salad, as that wilted globe cost over a dollar.

It was strange how quickly I became accustomed to the prices, but food was essential, and we made the necessary adjustments. Besides, we were still new, and everything in Alaska seemed bigger and more exciting than our life in Montana. The sun...oh, it was bright and shining almost twenty-four hours a day. The flowers were the biggest and the brightest I had ever seen. Plain old yellow or orange marigolds were twice the size of normal ones and twice as vivid. Everywhere you looked there were fireweed, Alaska cotton, Arctic poppies and other colorful flowers, whose names I didn't know.

Those long hours of sunshine not only made the flowers grow to an amazing brilliance and size, but also gave many people an unusual amount of energy. It was common to see people outside at midnight with small children playing instead of sleeping. If you went fishing in the middle of the night thinking you would have the river all to yourself, you were wrong. It seemed everyone had the same idea.

We quickly began looking for a place to live, either to buy or rent. It was a rather disheartening search as prices to us were totally outrageous. We knew everything would cost more there, but wow, not quite that much. The worst problem was that there weren't many places to rent or to buy.

Of course, everyone dreams of owning a quaint little log cabin when they think of living in Alaska. Well, those little log cabins were scarce or shockingly expensive to a newcomer. We didn't have the benefits of a double income yet, and we were still wet behind the ears about Alaskan life.

After a week of searching, we had found one sweet little house we both loved and could almost afford and one rather old trailer house (not a mobile home) we could well afford. We bought the trailer house. It was our first home purchase, and unbelievably, we found a bank that would happily lend us the money.

Settling into our trailer was easy. We had only a few possessions with us other than guns, fishing rods, our clothes, some household items, and whatever we could fit into our pickup's camper shell. Thankfully, our new home was furnished and ready to live in. We quickly reloaded our pickup with camping gear and started to explore the Last Frontier.

My research suggested then was one of the best times to see the Interior. The weather was supposed to be at its finest, and fishing was also at its best, both in the Interior and in all rivers of the entire state. Who wouldn't be excited to see this amazing place in all its glory?

We had two glorious days of camping along crystal-clear lakes and creeks, catching an amazing amount of grayling and even a small lake trout. Then the rains began. It rained and rained and rained. What about my research? Could I have made a mistake? Wasn't this supposed to be the best time to enjoy the perfect weather? I wasn't mistaken. This was just an unusual nasty weather front that had moved in, and it wasn't in a hurry to leave. Being on the back roads, the radio signals were rather limited, but the weather reports were for continued rain and possible flooding.

Stopping at different roadhouses along the highway, the conversations were all about the rain and possible flooding. Several of the old-time Alaskans were concerned that Fairbanks might flood. Although it seemed crazy to them, that was what they heard on their two-way radios. Being a little tired of sleeping in the wet camper and living in the rain, we headed back to our new home.

Arriving back in Fairbanks, we found our trailer house safe and dry. However, the owner of the court was filling sandbags with the help of all the renters. Unsure as to why they were doing this, we joined in and filled many sandbags. Within two days, we understood why we had helped with the sandbags. Lakeview Trailer Court, the University of Alaska, and the upper floors of the Northward Building were the only dry places in Fairbanks.

CHAPTER 3

# THE FLOOD OF 1967 HAD BEGUN

The rainfall for August 11-13 in Fairbanks was record-breaking. Normally, about two inches fell for the entire month. In 1967, it was recorded as 6.2 inches in five days.

The local radio and television stations were broadcasting flood warnings daily. Warnings became so common that soon people were ignoring the broadcasts. After all, the Chena river was a small, shallow, quiet river that meandered through the middle of town and wasn't much of a threat. However, on August 15, the Chena left its banks at 18.6 feet and headed rapidly through town towards the Tanana River.

Even with the daily warnings, people in Fairbanks were taken by complete surprise. Once the Chena escaped its banks, it roared through the entire city. With the river bearing down on them, people were left with nowhere to go. All highways were closed! All commercial air traffic was stopped. There weren't any mountains or hills to climb to get out of the water. The highest spot around was the hillside of the University of Alaska. Rescue boats retrieved hundreds of stranded people, while others trekked to higher ground alone. Between seven and eight thousand people made their way to that one hilltop.

The university became an evacuation center for flood victims. Luckily, it had its own power plant, as there was no other power in the city. However, with water rising at two inches an hour, the power plant was being threatened with flooding. This lone building supplied water, heat, and electricity to well over seven thousand people.

The university radio station put out a broadcast asking for volunteers to fill sandbags. Sadly, only two men showed up. Then a second broadcast was made, and one person remembers it like this:

"It was like a caribou migration coming over the hill—men, women, and children by the hundreds. They grabbed shovels and waded into a long, long job of filling needed sandbags to save the power plant. It was a sight to behold."

Downtown at the Northward Building, the tallest building in Fairbanks, people had opened their apartments to evacuees. No one seemed to know how many people were gathered inside the seven floors above the flood waters, but many good stories came from the Northward Building evacuation center. It was said that the Northward bar and liquor store cleared its shelves and dispensed booze to one and all.

While we were filling our sandbags to keep the water back from Lakeview Trailer Court and our new home dry, we didn't know the above news until much later. All we knew was that all roads in the Fairbanks area were closed. This warning was broadcast on every radio and television station. The owner of our trailer court posted news bulletins in his office for hourly updates.

Strangely, we watched people in big four-wheel-drive trucks come charging down the street and crash over the sandbags. They would proceed maybe two hundred feet, and their truck would sputter to a stop and start floating into deeper water, and then they swam back to where they had just left. This happened several times until the owner of the court erected a fence to stop the crazy people. I was never sure where they thought they were going, but I guess it was out of pure fear. If the sandbags didn't keep back the rising river, there was absolutely nowhere to go, unless you had a boat.

Being fishermen, we did have a boat and motor, which we tied to our trailer house in case the sandbags failed. We took turns doing flood watch throughout the night. Hub gave me orders to wake him, quickly load our supplies, get into the boat, and remember to grab the guns, if I saw water over the road or heard the emergency siren. Okay, that didn't happen, but it was the conversation between us for two days and two extremely long nights.

Every day he would give me the same instructions: if we had to take the boat, I was supposed to take two guns for our protection. Yes, for protection from other people without a boat or those trying to get into our boat. Every day it was the same conversation, and I would tell him, "I sure as hell am not going to shoot someone to keep them away from the damned boat." I guess everyone must have gotten a bit crazy in the flood, or that was my excuse for his irrational thinking.

After a few days, the floods started to subside. The Red Cross brought in food and water. Everyone was given tetanus and typhoid shots because of the amount of sewage that had been released. Plus, there were rats everywhere. People were celebrating their safety and their dry homes, and nothing else mattered. Well, there were still many complaints about the rats, the cockroaches, and the horrid stench.

About this time, we heard on the news that one downtown grocery store was open. Into our boat we went, and motored all the way into town which was close to six miles. It was an incredibly horrific sight. There would be a roof of a house peeking out, or we would see a car or truck totally under water. We followed what we thought was the highway into town, guided along the submerged roadway by the trees, which were almost covered by water. Traveling down the main street of Fairbanks, we pulled up to the grocery store in our boat. In that part of town, you could see some streets draining dry and a few cars driving somewhere. I've no idea what we bought. I think we did it for the adventure, not from a need of food.

One week after the entire city had been under water, most stores were already opening. That same week I applied for a job and was hired at the new JC Penny's beauty salon. Clean water was bought from a water truck, and we gave cold shampoos. Then a brilliant person brought us a Coleman camp stove to heat the water. No matter how primitive it was, we were open for business, and the ladies stood waiting in line.

This big new store had been completely under water, with clothes floating down the street, the week before. That was how the entire town came back to life. Hoses, pumps, shovels, and brooms were used to hurry and get things clean before freeze-up arrived. Throughout the whole town, you would see people pulling up carpets, using their garden hoses to flush the mud and sewage away. The local people of each block swept and washed their street. It was incredible to see how quickly everything returned to normal. However, years later in many homes, the marks on the walls where the water had risen still remained and would pop through no matter how many coats of paint were applied.

Oh, about the little house that we wanted to buy, but couldn't afford: sadly it washed away in the flood. It sure made me appreciate my old trailer house.

Fairbanks returned to the little town of thirteen thousand people living life like the flood had never happened, and we did the same. We had gone there to live an Alaskan life, and we were determined to do it!

CHAPTER 4
# FROZEN WHAT?

When you wake up in the morning and it's sixty below zero, you have to wonder why anyone wants to live in Alaska, but we did, and we loved every moment of it, flood and all.

We had gotten lucky and survived the Great Fairbanks flood, safe and dry in our home-on-wheels at Lakeview Trailer Court. BUT…

I have to say that life in this little home could stress the best of Alaskan women. When the temperature reached thirty to sixty degrees below zero outside, it was only a few degrees warmer inside our not-so-cozy home. Perhaps that's a slight stretch of the truth, but you certainly had to wear a sweater at all times. Bedtime was welcomed each night for the comfort of an electric blanket and a down comforter. These lovely bedcovers still didn't protect you from a frozen nose but did allow you to sleep in warmth.

Our little home, like any trailer built then, wasn't noted for its insulation benefits. Every morning when I opened my clothes closet, I would carefully pry my clothes from the block of ice that had developed inside. The first time I was greeted by this dilemma, I thought maybe my dress had snagged on a nail, and I cautiously pushed the other dresses aside to discover my nemesis. It took a few minutes for my brain to register what the white, cold object I could feel was… ice! How can you have ice inside a house?

I removed my clothes from the closet and slowly chipped about five pounds of this frozen mass away. I decided I had to leave the closet door open and let it warm up a little, but then what? The dress I planned to wear was still frozen; in fact, all my clothes were either frozen or slightly damp.

Using my hair dryer, I quickly solved the problem with my clothes, but what could I do about the closet? Later at work, I asked my coworkers for their advice. After everyone had a good laugh, no one had much to offer. I knew I needed some insulation, but I couldn't use that horrid fiberglass stuff. The hardware store recommended some Styrofoam sheets, which sounded easy and practical. So I spent the evening in my closet, cutting and gluing Styrofoam to my wall. It seemed like a good idea at the time..

About a week later, curled up under my cozy bedcovers, I heard *pop, pop, crack.* It sounded as if someone was knocking on the side of the house, but no one was outside when I went to check. This same noise continued periodically throughout the night. In the morning, when I opened the closet door, my clothes were all pushed aside, and the Styrofoam had broken into small pieces. A massive iceberg had formed again under my insulation. My final solution was to hang my clothes on a rope across the bedroom and hope it warmed up so I could clean up the mess of the now-frozen insulation and new ice.

After this little mess was cleaned up and the temperature rose, I discovered a crack in the side of my closet leading to the outside. I bought a can of spray insulation, filled the gap, and prayed that would be the end of my icy closet. Yes, problem solved. My clothes were still darn cold, but no more ice invaded my life.

Another quirky little thing I had to deal with in our trailer was when I plugged an electrical appliance into the socket; I had to do this slowly so the ice could melt. The first time I thought it was a messed-up plug because it just wouldn't go into the socket. I kept pushing and hearing a sizzling noise, but then it worked. I'm still amazed I never got a shock or blew a fuse. I patiently learned how to hold the plug and then gently push it into the electric socket until it fried its way through the icy outlet. Finally, I would hear my coffeepot perking away or my hairdryer working as if this were normal.

If you have a frozen closet and ice in the electrical outlets, you certainly should expect more problems. So that we weren't further disappointed, one Sunday morning, our drains in the bathroom didn't work. Our neighbor advised us that perhaps the heat tape to these pipes was no longer connected or may have been broken. Under Hub's direction, I scooted under the trailer to see what was happening. You do know Hub was much too big to crawl into that small space, and I would have been able to do this so much more easily than him, or so I was told.

With a flashlight in hand, I slowly crawled on my tummy into this mass of cobwebs, mouse droppings, and nasty dark crawl-space filled with pipes and electrical wires. Finally, I found where the bathroom drains were, and yes, it was covered in ice. Luckily, I found the heat tape that was no longer connected to the drain. I plugged it back into the circuit, crawled out of the dungeon, and within a few hours, the drains were working. Then Hub and I had a small discussion on who was to do what with any other problem underneath that blankety-blanking trailer.

I overcame the trials and traumas of our home rather well, but having a vehicle in the frozen north was no easy matter either. We had a head bolt heater installed, which all vehicles in Fairbanks needed. This was an electric apparatus to warm the engine, and you needed to remember to plug it in, or you were headed for a truck/car that wouldn't start. After forgetting this one time, I posted notes everywhere as a nightly reminder: 'Plug in pickup before bed.' During the day, I would start our pickup a couple of times or more a day, depending on the temperature. At sixty below zero, this wasn't fun, and the least discomfort you got was a frozen hinny.

Our truck wasn't an automatic, so you also had to remember to leave it in neutral, not in gear. If you forgot, you were stuck with the extra effort of holding the clutch in until the engine and gears warmed and a super-frozen butt. I forgot more than once and suffered the consequences.

Some schools, businesses, and malls had plug-in sockets for head bolt heaters, but if not, it was crucial to get that vehicle running before it froze up. Where I worked, there wasn't such a thing. This led to everyone taking a break, not for coffee, but to start the engines.

Then of course, there was the dreaded frostbite. I clearly remember my frostbitten ear, because I still have signs of it to this day. I was preparing for a polar-bear hunt, and I needed to make sure that my gun functioned at severe temperatures. It was definitely cold enough: around forty-five below zero with a slight breeze. They didn't record chill factor back then, but no matter what, I registered it as damn cold. My ears were covered with a knitted stocking cap, and I had my parka hood up. However, to shoot accurately, I had to pull my hood down, so only the stocking cap was covering my ears. After two quick shots, I jumped back in the pickup, and it already felt as if my one ear had severe sunburn. Later, the skin on the top of my ear peeled off and became permanently discolored. I did learn that my gun could shoot under severe cold temperatures, and that ears can freeze extremely fast.

CHAPTER 5
# THOSE ELUSIVE NORTHERN LIGHTS

*Oh, it was wild and weird and wan, and ever in camp o' nights*
*we would watch and watch the silver dance of the mystic Northern*
*Lights*
Hugh D'Arcy

Many years ago, while still in high school, I saw what I thought might be the end of the world—or maybe a view of heaven. While parked with my boyfriend on the hillside overlooking town, we stopped playing kissy-face and noticed a glow of lights in the sky. This little glow turned into a golden circle with red and blue encasing it. Then it became a large bright circle of flickering light. It scared me so much, all I wanted to do was go home and see my family, thinking the next thing that happen might be my death, or that I would be transported to an alien ship.

I did hurry home. I woke my parents and told them what I had seen. My father rolled over and said, "Oh, don't worry that was probably just the northern lights. Your mom and I saw a nice show of them earlier tonight. I don't think you're ready for heaven, or maybe heaven isn't ready for you." That was the end of that discussion, and with time I forgot how spectacular it had been.

I knew the northern lights—also called the aurora borealis—could be seen in Alaska, but whenever I remembered to watch for them, disappointingly, they were never there. Then one night, as I stepped outside to empty the garbage, like magic there they were. Suddenly, they were right before my eyes, and I didn't even know what they were.

I was taken aback by what I first thought was lightning, but it couldn't have been lightning when it was thirty below zero. So I kept walking, but then I heard a noise that sounded like electrical wires buzzing. Being a little nervous and fearing a power line was coming down, I stopped. When I looked up again, there was a rapid streak of light. I kept watching, even though I was freezing, and icicles were forming on the end of my dripping nose. Above me, there came a quick flash of green, yellow, and pink ribbons dancing a tango. Within seconds, the colors changed and moved across the sky. What was there one moment disappeared and reappeared again but with different colors. I knew I would stay, if I let myself, until I froze because these lights were so incredible. After a while, I ran inside to tell my husband to hurry and come outside. Well, by the time I did, it was the end of the show, and there was nothing left to see. He wasn't happy that I had dragged him into the freezing cold for nothing more than frozen nose hairs.

Throughout the years, he came to understand how fast the lights could arrive and disappear. Many times, we heard their electric noises while viewing their pink, green, blue, purple, white, magical, and swirling dance while living in the quietness of the Brooks Range or alongside a quiet road. They were always a shocking surprise no matter how many times I saw them. The electric noise was an unusual and added treat. Sadly, many people living in the city, where it's too noisy, never experience the incredible sound of the northern lights.

I have also seen the man-made aurora created by scientists, but they failed miserably compared to Mother Nature and her glorious treats for those fortunate enough to see and hear the real thing. Many people say the best time for viewing the aurora borealis is in September, but I think the best time is whenever it decides to appear and do its magical dance.

CHAPTER 6
# CARIBOU, THE ALASKAN GHOSTS

Some people might imagine Alaska has a moose behind every tree or one walking the main street of town. I'm sorry to disappoint, but it isn't true. Other people might think Alaskans live in igloos: not true either, but they make a cute picture. I imagined thousands of caribou tromping across the tundra, running from a pack of wolves on every hillside. I thought with over nine hundred fifty thousand caribou in Alaska, they would be on every hill or valley. This would have been true if you were lucky enough to be in the right place at the right time.

After living in Fairbanks for three or four months, snow had fallen, winter had begun, and I had yet to see a caribou. Then came the highly anticipated report that the caribou were migrating onto the Steese Highway. Filled with excitement, we loaded our truck and headed out for our first caribou hunt.

This was a rather expensive hunt because we weren't Alaskan residents yet and had to purchase non-resident licenses and specific tags for hunting caribou. We weren't the only ones anticipating this reported migration, and the farther up the Steese we went, the more hunters we encountered. As the snow got deeper, the highway became impassable with trucks stuck every which way on the road. It became more of a 'helping people dig their rigs out' than a hunting expedition.

The Department of Fish and Game had reported that thousands of caribou were in this area, but where were they? It appeared we had all missed the migration; maybe we weren't in the right spot, or with all the noise from the digging party perhaps we had scared the caribou away.

Not wanting to give up, we put on our snowshoes, hoping to climb up to a ridge high above the other hunters and away from the noise of revved engines and angry voices. With thousands and thousands of caribou in Alaska, you would have thought we could have found one, wouldn't you? After trekking about for the rest of the day, we returned to our truck without seeing neither hide nor hair of a single caribou.

Not to be stopped, we returned at daybreak the following day. We had succeeded in making it to the summit before other vehicles became stuck and blocked the road. Once again, we put on our snowshoes and headed to a ridge farther away from the road. As the sun rose higher in the morning sky, we saw movement in the trees. As the light became brighter, we could see a trail, and on that trail were four caribou.

They appeared like ghosts; at first we could see them, and then they were gone. Quick flashes of movement were all I could glimpse. I wasn't even sure they were caribou—maybe it was just my imagination. We kept climbing over the next ridge, following the trail the caribou had beaten through the snow. When the trail climbed out of the trees and led to open ground, like magic, the entire hillside looked like an anthill; only this hill was filled with caribou.

We plopped onto our bellies and watched through our scopes as they moved along, eating, trotting, eating, moving, always moving. It was an incredible sight to see, with at least a hundred or more caribou right before our eyes. Hub whispered that there were two or three big bulls with double shovels, and he was ready to take one. He took his shot, and I saw one go down. Then the entire hillside seemed in motion with caribou trotting out of my view. His caribou was a magnificent double shovel, and I was a little envious and sorry I hadn't done the same.

Hub asked, "Why didn't you take a shot? You'll never get a better or closer shot than that. I can't believe you didn't even take a shot. There were probably more big bulls in that herd than you could imagine, and still you didn't shoot."

I could tell he was a little irritated, so I finally said, "Well, if we both used our tag today that would be the end of our hunt for the year, and you sure wouldn't like that, would you?" The truth was more like, *I just got so caught up in the thrill of watching them, I forgot to shoot.* Seeing hundreds of caribou on that hillside was exactly what I had imagined, and it was better than any shot I could have taken that day.

Within a few minutes, we could hear a lot of shooting coming from the direction of our pickup. As we dragged this incredible animal back to the truck, we saw several successful hunters alongside the road. We had to drag our animal about a mile, while the road hunters got lucky and had to go no more than fifty feet. To my way of thinking, that's not called hunting, but I guess their caribou would have tasted just as good as our hard-earned one.

Once Hub's caribou was loaded into the back end of our pickup, several other hunters came by for a viewing and a hearty congratulation. They were quite impressed that this was a good-sized double-shovel bull. A double shovel wasn't that rare back in 1967, but those antlers with the base having two instead of one shovel and tall main points were a highly sought-after bull.

I did take my first shot—and oops, I missed—a few weeks later on the Denali Highway out of Paxson. Over the years, this area became my favorite spot for caribou. It was mostly barren ground with large rolling hills and held the Nelchina herd, which numbered around forty thousand. It didn't have an abundance of hunters, and nice-sized bulls seemed to be plentiful. With the rolling hills, spotting a herd was usually easy and within walking distance. My first caribou came from this herd. It wasn't a double shovel, but it was still a respectable horn measurement of about five feet long, end to end.

Even though this took place almost fifty years ago, I remember this particular hunt as if it happened yesterday. We saw herds of twenty or thirty on many hillsides that day, but they were all moving farther away from us, except this one herd of about fifty. Hub had his spotting scope out and was closely watching the direction in which this herd was moving. We decided to make our move and try to get over the next hill before they arrived.

I was hurrying and hoping like crazy I would connect with my first caribou on that day. As we got to higher ground, we saw the herd had changed directions and were moving away from us. After taking a little rest, we then climbed to the next ridge, and there, like ghosts, was a herd of over a hundred perfectly spectacular caribou. I immediately plopped down on my belly, and both Hub and I were busy scoping out the nicest bull. I found the one I wanted at about a hundred and fifty yards, with nothing between me and him. I took my shot and then watched the other caribou trot off to safer ground. It was a long drag back to our truck, but it was so worth every minute. Throughout the years, the Nelchina herd supplied us with most of our delicious caribou meat and lots of exciting caribou hunts, but that first hunt was always the best.

Not only do caribou taste delicious, but their hides are the warmest and the most useful. Caribou hair is hollow, so the air trapped inside the hairs acts as insulation, making their hide a treasured item in Alaska. I found these hides made fantastic mukluks, blankets, or outdoor shelters, as not only were they warm but also waterproof. My mukluks were made by an Eskimo lady from Anaktuvuk Pass and were constructed from the back leg of a bull caribou; this being the biggest and thickest hide, it's the easiest from which to create footwear. She used light and dark colored caribou hair for the decoration of the top part of my mukluk, so not only were they toasty warm, but also pretty enough to wear anywhere in Alaska.

Three of the reasons I love to hunt caribou are not only are they good to eat and have majestic horns, but they're much easier to take care of afterwards than a huge Alaskan moose.

This is what I learned on my first Alaskan moose hunt: yes, they're breathtaking with their enormous bodies and incredibly large horns. However, that also becomes a problem after you've shot one. My moose was a lovely large bull, standing at the edge of a slough, quietly munching willows.

Hub and I had spotted him early that morning, and we waited patiently hoping he would move out of the water onto drier ground. I guess our patience ran out because we decided we had better take him soon in case he got our scent and left. I carefully aimed, took my shot, and this big old brute just threw his head up; a ton of willows flew into the air. I quickly reloaded and took another shot. This time he went down in a big splash of water.

Getting to the moose wasn't an easy job, as the water was much deeper than I thought, and the mud sucked me down to the top of my hip boots. Hub had left me to go back to the airplane to get a come-along (a hand-operated ratchet winch) that we would need to pull Mr. Moose out of the water onto higher ground. At this point, the fun had ended, and hard work was the order of the day.

After an hour of dragging this giant out of the water, we then spent a couple of hours butchering him. The first problem was just moving his head so we could remove his horns. Those suckers are huge and weigh around seventy pounds. So you know we had a first-class wrestling match on our hands. No matter what I did, that moose ended up on top of me, and I was losing the battle of escaping from his horns or his body. Finally, our moose was butchered, and we had won the battle of man against moose. This humongous animal would provide us with many delicious meals throughout the winter. Hub would return another day to retrieve the horns of this wonderful animal, and they would be proudly hung over our garage doors, like many good Alaskan hunters' homes.

## CHAPTER 7
# DALL SHEEP, GRIZZLY BEAR, AND MOOSE

Summers in Alaska were the reward for withstanding the dark cold winters, and we used them to their fullest.

Every June, after Hub had finished teaching for the year, I would also quit my job as a cosmetologist, and we would explore Alaska. In the summer of 1968, we spent over a month in the Brooks Range on the Hammond River, hunting, camping, and doing a little fishing.

This trip took a lot of planning, and Hub was a detailed planner. He chose the headwaters of the Hammond River for their remoteness and lack of hunters. The Brooks Range wasn't on the maps for the average hunter back then. In fact, most of the pilots we knew said it would be difficult to find anyone to fly us into that drainage.

Hub's persistence won out, and he found a well-respected pilot and cut a deal with him. Chuck Gray was a bush pilot extraordinaire and had flown the area since 1948. Talking with Chuck was like flying beside him over most of Alaska; his stories were so alive with adventure. This man clearly knew the Brooks Range, and we were lucky to have found him.

As we showed him the map and discussed our plans, Chuck told us, "I'm not familiar with that particular spot, but I don't see any problem as far as the flying goes. If that's where you want to go, I can do it. Landing on the Hammond is no different from any other river. I'm really not sure it's a good idea for a woman to be doing this trip, though." Being used to male chauvinists, I just smiled, and he continued with his questions. "Are you certain you want to spend more than a month there? You do know you'll be all alone, and if you have any trouble, no one will be there to help you out." We assured him that we were ready for this adventure and happy to have him for our pilot.

For the first stage of our journey, our friend, Brian Cleworth, would fly us and all our gear into Lake Chandalar. This lake lies about 60 miles north of the Arctic Circle and is about a ninety-minute flight from Fairbanks. In Brian's Cessna 180, it was an easy and picturesque flight.

This was the first time I had seen how vast the Brooks Range was. This mountain range forms the northernmost drainage divide in North America, separating streams flowing into the Arctic Ocean, the Bering Sea, the Gulf of Alaska, and the North Pacific. It stretches from west to east across northern Alaska and into Canada's Yukon Territory, a total distance of about 700 miles. Some of these mountains reach a height of 9,000 feet. Aside from statistics, it was incredible to fly for so long over never-ending hills and spectacular mountains. It seemed to me that as soon as we had crossed over the mighty Yukon delta, we were at the beginning of the vast Brooks Range.

Landing at Lake Chandalar was, to my way of thinking, a picture of what Alaska should look like forever. We saw a perfect clear-blue lake surrounded by mountains, and alongside the lake sat one lone elegant old log cabin. It was a photographer's dream. In my heart, I thought it was the most picturesque spot I had seen in Alaska.

Chuck Gray was waiting at the side of this lovely lake with his trusty Super Cub, ready to fly us into the headwaters of the Hammond River. As we transferred our supplies from Brian's 180 to the Super Cub, we also looked at maps and did a bit of serious talking. Chuck still wasn't too comfortable about taking a woman into such a remote area, but when I started loading his plane as the men were talking, he understood I was going whether he approved or not. What could he do? Leave me there? Did he think taking Hub alone would be a brilliant idea? He decided I would be his first passenger, because of weight, and we would only take a small, light load of supplies on this trip, as he was unsure of what he would find to land on.

Being excited to start this adventure, I jumped into Chuck's little Super Cub, buckled my seatbelt, and off we went into the wild blue yonder. Once in the air, he again warned me of being in this remote area with no help from the outside world. I assured him I wasn't concerned about being in the wilderness of Alaska all alone, and I didn't think I would need help from anyone other than Hub. I had been hunting and camping since I was eight years old. Why would this be any different?

Soon we were at the headwaters of the Hammond River, and as Chuck started flying lower and lower, I tightened my seat belt tighter and tighter. We were flying so low, it felt like I could reach out and pick the blueberries off their bushes, or grab the little birds flying by. Not only were we low, but we were flying so slowly, I thought I could probably run as fast as he was flying. At this point, I started to mentally question his flying skills and prepared to crash.

When he found a stretch of the river he was looking for, he did a couple of fly-bys and told me to keep watching for big boulders. I had no idea what he wanted me to do with these boulders if I did spot them, but I kept watching. The sandbar he chose to land on looked way too small to me, and I was then sure he was totally crazy. How could he possibly land there? I closed my eyes and hoped for the best. When the plane hit the ground, there was a bump, bump, and then we came to a quick stop. He landed us safely on his chosen sandbar. Sandbar is stretching it a lot; this was a rock bar with only big rocks and boulders. There was no sand anywhere, but it was good enough for Chuck and his Cub.

I guess he was in a hurry because as soon as I climbed out, he was throwing our gear right behind me. He gave me instructions to clear the boulders in the middle of where he had landed and to make the strip as long as possible. I was to mark where I had extended it with our tent on one end and something brightly colored on the other. He pitched a few boulders away from the front of the plane, jumped back in, and yelled that I needed to hurry and move lots of rocks, so he had a longer landing field because when he returned he would be carrying a much heavier load.

I did what I thought was needed: rolling the biggest boulders to the edge of the river as Chuck had directed. Not an easy task when those suckers weighed as much as I did. It seemed the more boulders I moved, the more there were. I finally pushed the biggest from the middle of his landing strip and then only had to improve the length.

After rolling and pitching rocks for what seemed like an hour, I finally heard the buzz, buzz, buzz of an airplane. Looking up into the sky, I couldn't see his plane, but when I stood up, the Super Cub was only ten feet or so above my head, if that. I had forgotten how low and slow this man and his plane could fly. I ran like hell to get off the so-called landing strip, and he came again, giving me just enough time to get up the river bank. Then I got to watch this bush pilot perform his sandbar (rock and boulder bar) landing to perfection. I didn't know how short a strip he could land on, but I did know how low and slow he could fly. I guess what I had created was good enough, as he landed without a problem. He quickly threw more of our gear onto the ground and took off again to return with Hub and the final load.

Later, after we had unloaded the last load, Chuck asked me, "Were you thinking I wasn't a very good pilot and needed the whole riverbank to land? I think a 747 could land on what you cleared. Nice work, though, because now I don't have to worry about a headwind, and I can just take off anywhere. I'll be back six weeks from today. If not on that day, be ready every day thereafter. It all depends on the weather, but don't worry, I'll pick you up as soon as possible." Then he gave us a wave and climbed back into his plane.

I swear he took off in maybe ten or fifteen feet. He cranked his engine until it sounded like it might shake apart. Then I saw the tail end of the Cub lift up, and within a few feet, he was airborne. He did a quick turnaround, flew over us, dipped a wing, and was over the treetops and out of sight within a few seconds. He became my hero of the day, and I was positive he had to be the best bush pilot on the North American continent.

We had done it. There we were on the headwaters of the Hammond River, the most remote area Hub could find with prime hunting for Dall sheep and one of the most primitive areas of the United States.

We set up our camp on the bank above the river, high enough in the event of rain and the river rising, but close enough to fetch water with ease. Even though we planned to be there for over a month, our camp didn't take long to set up because we had minimum gear with us. It was interesting for me to see what Hub had packed for several weeks of camping. I had been at work until the day before we left, so he had done everything himself.

I knew we had to keep our weight to a minimum, as Chuck had told us earlier, but the supplies seemed alarmingly minimal. We did have a decent tent, two sleeping bags, a small Coleman camp stove with a five-gallon can of (Blazo) white gas, two guns with a box of twenty shells for each gun, a spotting scope, two backpacks, a hatchet, one plastic collapsible pail, and several hefty plastic bags. Where was the food? This was *not* looking good to me. All we had were several tinfoil packets of dehydrated food. This was nutritional at best; most of it tasted like a strange chemical rather than food. There were lots of packets of stew, a few packs of dried scrambled eggs, and some dried vegetables of various sorts. Oh yes, we had several little cans of Vienna sausage, which Hub knew I wouldn't eat unless I was starving, and one can of Spam for me. There were a few onions, two plastic containers of eggs, and a bag of potatoes for real food. I had packed my female supplies, a carton of cigarettes, and a box of candy bars. I knew the cigarettes and candy had to be separated, or a holy fight would take place because Hub would abscond with much more than his half. I quickly took my cigarettes and candy and sneaked off to hide my goodies. I dug a little hole under the tundra and made my stash where I thought it would be secure from bears, varmints, and Hub.

The first few days were spent making our camp like a little home. We had hung all our food in bags high in the tall Alder tree beside our camp (called bear-proofing). This made cooking a not-so-easy chore of hoisting it up and down for every meal, which was a big pain, but it was better than having bears in our camp. Then we had a daily water-carrying exercise from the creek. It's surprising how much water is needed for drinking and cleaning. Shockingly, by today's standards, we never even boiled our water but drank it straight from the river. I'm sure that's no longer recommended.

After our little chores were completed, we spent the rest of the day playing cards, swatting mosquitoes, chatting about our hunt, swatting more mosquitoes, and doing whatever we wanted. Then we both decided we needed to see what was near and far from our camp. We spent several days exploring the hillsides and spotting for Dall sheep on the mountainsides.

Our camp was a fair hike to where we felt the mountainside would offer a chance to spot sheep. We had intentionally kept away from where we thought the best location would be for animal activity. We didn't want to disrupt the normal route the sheep in our area would travel. On the first day away from camp, we spotted a small herd of ewes and kids. Farther away from this same area, we caught a glimpse of a small ram, and that was a promising sign of bigger rams. It was the time of year when the ewes and kids stuck together and the rams separated into their own herd. A rather chauvinistic group, the rams only join the ewes during November and December for mating, and then they regroup once again into their male-only society. Spotting a small ram gave us hope of a bigger, legal one.

We would walk upriver a couple of miles or more each day to a little hillside, where we could watch the mountain for sheep. We would lie on the ground all day, with our eyes glued to the mountainside, where we had seen the little ram. We would take turns with the spotting scope, looking until our eyeballs ached. It was going to be a hard climb once we spotted the group we hoped for, and we wanted to make sure they were back on this hillside before starting our beastly ascent.

A few days later, we again spotted our little ram in the early morning and knew it was when he normally fed in the lower areas. Two or three more sheep stood below him, happily grazing. We couldn't see if they were legal, full-curl rams or not, but we assumed there had to be a big one hiding in there somewhere. If what we had observed and read about Dall sheep was true, this group should have fed on the lower grassy slopes in the morning hours. By midmorning, they should have started their way back up into the rocky hillside where they would spend the day bedded down.

We had started out very early in the morning, at 5:00 a.m., with only a quick cup of coffee and a dry hard biscuit. We trudged upriver at least a couple of miles, jumping across small creeks and dodging the many little slews just to get to our daily spotting area. Then we would march through the lowland tundra to begin the brutal climb to the top of this steep, craggy mountain. The walk through the boggy tundra felt like walking on a wet sponge and then playing a jumping game from one dry spot to the next. Each step I took was exhausting because I kept sinking into the muskeg or had to jump from hummock to hummock and would slip into small bogs of water. If my legs were already tired, how would they ever carry me up that steep, steep side of Apoon Mountain with an elevation of seven thousand feet?

As I looked to the peak, many questions ran through my mind. How could we hide ourselves for an hour or two? Could I actually climb all the way to the top of this monster? Could I be so quiet that they wouldn't hear us? Could I make the perfect shot and not have a wounded animal to track? I hoped my years of hunting and the many hours of target practice would pay off, but I also knew my smoking habit would make that climb a killer.

These were private little questions at the beginning of our climb. As the mountain became steeper, with only a handful of grass to grab and a few boulders to rest behind, I knew I would never make it to the top. We would rest and whisper to each other. Hub kept encouraging me to keep going, and then he promised that if I kept going, I would get the first shot, no matter what. Being a hunter and a determined woman, I couldn't quit. Giving in to anything short of a heart attack was out of the question.

Slowly, inch by inch, we were getting to the summit. We took a long rest to stop our racing hearts and load our guns before we broke over the top. My heart was pounding, not only from the climb but with the excitement of the hunt. As we lay there ready to load our guns, I looked to my right, and there stood an amazing big full-curl

Dall ram. Oh, yes, he was most definitely a full-curl and magnificent. My mind was racing with the thought of what to do. I didn't know if he had seen us and would then vanish.

Should I load my gun, or just lie still and hope he would stay close by? I couldn't stand the thought of missing this one opportunity for a perfect shot. I slowly moved my hand to load a shell, knowing it would break the silence. As I jacked a shell into the chamber of my .350 Remington Winchester magnum, the metallic clamor broke the surrounding quietness like a slamming of a car door on a cold winter night. Even to my ears, it was a noise to run away from. Yes, he had heard the noise and was gone. Then like magic, he was standing on a ledge directly above me. I took my shot, and down he fell, careening off the ledge and onto the shale below dropping, sliding, and then crashing almost at our feet.

Hub was as excited as if it was his sheep. He kept telling me what a great shot it was and how all those years of target practice had really paid off. Then he offered more congratulations on never quitting on the brutal climb up Apoon. Pictures were taken, and finally we sat with my sheep on the rocky pinnacle below the summit to have our first cigarette. We sat quietly together, admiring the beauty of my ram and viewing the deep green valley far below. It was by far more perfect than I imagined when I was whining about the difficulty of climbing this mountain.

As we sat, happy with our conquest, Hub started to recite his favorite poem: '*What drives a hunter onward, ever forward until at last he's forced to rest?*' He was so involved in his recital, he hadn't seen the huge ram standing watching us. Out of the corner of my mouth, I kept whispering to him to shut up and poking him in the ribs, but still he went on: '*Is it sight of moose, or bear or ram, or born of a hunter's lust?*' Finally, I poked him so hard, he became irritated enough to look over at me and saw the ram standing right in front of us. He slowly bent down to pick up his rifle. The ram was still standing looking at us, and then it made a lunge to a higher cliff. That was the pause Hub needed, and *boom* went his rifle. Down came the ram, falling, falling, and falling off the cliff. When it finally came to a stop, I think the only thing not broken, bruised, or tenderized, were its magnificent horns. Sitting and gazing at these magnificent animals, Hub continued: '*To see a lordly rack of horns, crash in the bloody dust.*'

Now, we clearly had a big job on our hands. We had come prepared for one sheep if we got lucky. Both of us carried a packboard, a jug of water, some rope, and our rifles, but we hadn't planned on taking two sheep in one day. I wasn't too concerned about the weight of the animal and thought it had to be about the same weight of a mule deer. My plan was to butt-scoot down the steepest part of the mountain and hope the shale would keep me moving. Once we were off the shale slide, we could stop and take care of the meat, or so I thought.

When my sheep was tied on the packboard, I changed my mind about how easy this was going to be. This animal weighed about two hundred pounds or more, and his horns poked my side or hit me in the head, no matter how he was tied. Hub didn't think much of my butt-scooting technique, but it was all I could do. I couldn't stand up and walk down the death-defying slope. I did well in the shale while it slid along with me and kept me and my sheep moving. The noise the shale and I made was like a huge avalanche of crashes and giggles. When the shale area stopped, so did I.

We then had a debate about what to do next. I won, simply because I was smaller and not as strong. I couldn't carry this critter across the tundra. We untied my pack and started to remove the head, which had been poking me all the way down the rockslide. We agreed we would carry the heads to the nearest tree, hang them up so they couldn't be eaten, and return for the rest of the sheep. Once the heads were both taken care of, we had to climb back up the mountain for the rest of the sheep.

Still early in the day, we decided to take care of the meat under the shade of a large pine tree. We skinned both animals, rolled their hides with the horns into the plastic bags we had with us, and hoisted them back up into the treetop. With just the meat on my back, I could easily manage my pack, and we started our long walk home.

We spent the rest of the day and well into the evening cutting up meat and digging a hole for storage. We dug a deep hole down to the permafrost (frozen ground) to use as a refrigerator. This meat was hopefully going to last us a couple of weeks, which was wonderful because I was already tired of eating dehydrated food that tasted of nothing. After we had cut the meat up and dealt with its storage, I heated water to clean up. Totally exhausted, we crashed for the night.

Waking up early to the smell of coffee brewing was a pure delight, but how I wished to be able to rest my weary body for the day. I felt like I had run a mile with a ton on my back. I thought this must be how elderly people felt each morning.

No rest was allowed that day because we had to recover the rest of our sheep, so I rolled out of the tent. After a cup or two of coffee, we headed back to where we had hung our sheep capes and horns. It didn't seem quite as far that morning as it did the evening before. It was good to see they were still safely hanging as we had left them. We spent a while just sitting under the shade of this lovely tree and admiring our rams' horns. Then, we both did a little bragging, and I poked some fun at the poet. It was a fun and peaceful morning, and we were in no hurry to get back to camp.

Walking on the edge of the Hammond was like strolling down a country lane, with the meandering river at our feet and a well-used animal trail to follow. As we came around the bend in the river, Hub stopped and said quietly, "Smell that stink. There's a bear close by, so load your gun, and be ready if something happens." We both watched the shrubs, and everything looked okay. We weren't sure whether to be as quiet or as loud as possible, but our plan was to get the hell out of that area quickly. We decided to cross the river as soon as it looked shallow enough to cross and get some space between us and the smell of bear.

We hurried along watchfully, but as we came around the next bend in the trail, there was Mr. Grizzly right in front of us. He wasn't more than a hundred feet away. He immediately reared up on his back legs and gave a roar that scared me to death. Hub had told me earlier to get rid of my pack and move away from it if we did run into a bear because we would smell like sheep, and bear love sheep. So, the first thing I did was drop my packboard and start backing up the trail. This was such a remote area, I'm sure this bear had never smelled a human before, but Mr. Grizzly either liked our smell or didn't like our looks. He was roaring and tossing his head from side to side, and his front legs were clawing the air frantically.

Hub started yelling his lungs out and flapping his arms to see if he could scare him away. Then he yelled at me, "Get ready to shoot if he doesn't turn around." Within seconds, the bear was down and coming at us. Hub fired his huge .264 Winchester Magnum, and I shot my big supposed-to-be bear gun, a .350 Magnum. Both guns nailed the bear in the chest and made him spin around. Up he came up again on his back legs, and this time he was one extremely pissed-off bear. We both fired again, and they were good solid hits. Once more he was knocked down, but still he was clawing the ground, tearing up small trees and dirt. He never quit his frightening bellowing. He was so close that we were being hit by his blood and foam spraying into the air.

Then, he dragged himself towards us on all fours, roaring and screaming, like no sound I had ever heard. He was still tossing his massive head from side to side, and his huge paws were throwing rocks and bushes aside. Within seconds, he was only about twenty feet away. We each had only one shell left, and that would be the end of our efforts to stop him. He was so close, all I could see with my scope was hair, and I wasn't sure where to aim, so I just took my last shot and saw it had at least spun his head away. A split second later, I heard Hub's gun go off and saw the bear stop.

Thankfully, that giant head was still, and his horrid roars were quiet. I was still backing up the trail and trying to load more shells, but I knew we didn't have time to load another shell if he was alive. How could he be alive? We had hit him six times with large caliber rifles, but I wasn't going to get any closer to find out. Finally, we were sure he was dead, and we had to hope there weren't any other bears around. We left him where he lay, reloaded our guns, picked up our packs, crossed the river, and quickly got the hell out of there.

We had two sheep hides to flesh out and take care of, plus an ugly, stinky, scary grizzly bear we had to go back to and skin. Our personal hunting code was: if you shoot it, you take care of the animal, and so we did. This bear stank so much, I could hardly hold a leg while Hub skinned it. Then we had to wrestle its hide back to camp, and that was unbelievably difficult. It seemed to slip and slide out of our carrying bag no matter what we did with it. All I wanted was to bury the smelly hide, and please, Hub, don't ask me to cook any of the meat. That wasn't going to happen if I had anything to say about it. Hub insisted we had to preserve the hide and at least eat some of the meat. Have you ever eaten grizzly bear meat? It's very, very greasy with a strong wild flavor at best and as tough as shoe leather. I would rather eat grubs, muktuk, or any other slimy greasy food.

The next couple of days were spent fleshing out our sheep capes, salting them down, and drying them in the sun. We checked our meat daily to make sure it didn't spoil. If there was any danger of it going bad, we would dry it for jerky. We had delicious meals of fresh sheep meat, and I thought it was the best wild meat in the world. Although I didn't like it, we also had to deal with the damned bear.

This was a big barren ground grizzly, although I've no idea what his official measurements were. When he stood, shaking his head from side to side and roaring at us, he made Hub look like a small man. Hub is over six feet tall, and this bear was more than that and twice as wide. When we laid its hide over the big boulders along the riverbank, it dwarfed everything around it. His head was so huge and heavy, it was all I could do to lift it. His fur was severely matted, and the color ranged from light brown to blonde. His stench was like rotten fish combined with a garbage dump. How he could smell so awful, I've no idea, but it was terrible.

I despised this ugly critter. I was angry that he had died, and just looking at him lying there scared me. To this day, I still remember him, so close, so loud, and so *I'm going to kill you and then eat you.* Then I had to sit and scrape the fat and flesh from his stinking hide. It took days, and everything I touched was greasy and smelly. I believe Hub must have sneaked a ton of salt aboard the plane. I had no idea we had that much salt and so little food. We salted Mr. Grizzly and rolled his hide into a canvas bag every night, and during the day, he was laid out in the sun to dry. It seemed that every day we had to do something with him, and quite frankly, I just wished he had never entered my life.

We were finally finished with the nasty bear, and instead of a cold bath in the river, I heated water for a small but halfway-cleansing bath. I had almost gotten used to washing my hair and body in the cold water, sleeping on pine boughs, eating jerky soup, and not much of anything else. I hadn't gotten used to the incessant presence of mosquitoes, the red welts they left on my body…or rather, my slightly dirty body. Even the heated water didn't help much; my fingernails were still black with dirt and bear grease, and neither of us had the nice fresh smell of a good warm shower. My cranky side was beginning to show, and home sweet home was looking damned good to me.

Now I had a new irritation: somewhere out there, a forest fire was beginning to make breathing a real problem. The smoke got worse daily, and that was all Hub wanted to talk about. Personally, I like to look on the positive side and prefer not to worry, but I do like to breathe. The air was much fresher along the river, so I decided it was time to fish.

The fishing was rather disappointing, and looking back, I blame the bear for that too. I'm sure that my hooks and gear all smelled of bear. More accurately, there probably weren't many grayling in the river in that particular area. I will admit that after meeting up with Mr. Grizzly, I wasn't too keen on walking through the trees along the creek banks in search of a good fishing hole. I decided that our camp was much safer, so I spent most of my time around the campfire checking our meat-drying rack, washing clothes, and trying to get rid of the greasy bear fat off them. Hours and hours were eaten away by playing cribbage, honeymoon pinochle, and arguing about who was the winner for the day.

Oh yes, Hub had packed plenty of salt, but not enough food, and by week five we were getting pretty darn short on groceries. We had eaten all the sheep meat and had made jerky from some of the bear, but we were down to almost nothing. We foraged for edible wild onions, greens, berries, or anything we could identify, but it wasn't like going to the supermarket.

Besides being concerned about food, the air was getting smokier by the day. With ten more days before we were scheduled to be picked up, the smoke had become so thick we couldn't see across the river. The sky was dark, and the smell grew stronger daily. Hub thought he should shoot the calf moose that lived across the river. He thought we might need the extra food, and then he started to seriously warn me about the fire. His concern was that if the fire broke over the hill, we would have to keep ahead of it and try to move to wetter ground. I understood what he was hinting at, and it seemed close to ludicrous to me. My concern was…ha-ha, there was no way we could ever walk out of there, even if we had lobster and steak airdropped into us. If Chuck Gray in his mighty Super Cub couldn't get in, we were totally screwed, moose meat or not.

With his deep concern about the fire and survival, he made the decision to shoot the calf because there was no way we could ever take care of the meat from the cow, as she was just too huge. He crossed the river and told me to be sure to keep my scope on the cow and watch for bear at the same time. He quickly shot the little calf, and was ready to start dragging it to camp when the mama cow burst through the trees. I could see she was going to trample Hub in about ten seconds. I shot, and she fell about five feet from the calf and Hub.

As we sat looking at our fine mess, Hub quietly admitted, "If you hadn't shot when you did, she would have killed me. She was so close, I felt the ground shake when she fell. I'm sure glad you're a good shot, or I'd be dead now. Do you know how many people die from being trampled by moose? Think how embarrassing that would be, but you'd sure have a great story to tell about your dead husband." All I could think was: we certainly had an abundance of moose meat.

We took the calf back to camp and took care of the meat. We would go over to the cow every day and cut off as much meat as we could make jerky from or cut into steaks. Moose meat was our meal for breakfast, lunch, and dinner. We kept a fire going day and night, making jerky. I guess Hub thought if we made enough jerky, it might save our lives. He had eaten so much jerky in the past month, his front teeth became loose. I preferred my jerky slightly boiled in a broth, which made it much easier to chew.

Hub kept warning me that he didn't think Chuck could get through this smoke. It was getting close to the departure time, so we got busy cleaning up our campsite. Neither of us felt very positive about leaving on the scheduled date. We did as Chuck had asked, and we were ready to go on the morning of our agreed date. The only thing left to do was take the tent down, which could be done while the first load was being shuttled to Chandalar Lake.

We solemnly sat on the riverbank all morning, quietly listening for the drone of an airplane. It wasn't looking too promising because we were still in a deep shroud of smoke. Around noon, the smoke lifted a little, and we had a nice breeze with some good fresh air. At about one o'clock, we heard a buzz, and that little Super Cub dropped out of the smoke-filled sky. As soon as I heard the plane, I ran to my hidden stash. I only had one pack of cigarettes left, but Hub had been without for several days. I knew I had one and only one cherished candy bar left. I had dreamed about eating it for several days, but I had kept it hidden for the perfect time or for the savior of starvation. It was the last one of my stash, and I was going to devour it with great joy. As I was digging up my prize, Hub tackled me, grabbed my candy bar, and the rotten SOB shoved the whole thing in his mouth.

At that moment, I wished that the moose had trampled him. Seeing how truly angry I was, he promised me a pound of candy bars and anything else I ever wanted. Laughing and eating MY candy bar, he confessed, "I was really scared we wouldn't be picked up, and we would never make it out of here alive." My thoughts were: *Too bad the bear didn't eat you or the moose trample you, you rotten candy-bar thief.*

After a lot of laughing, high-fiving, and hugging Chuck, we loaded the plane. I was the first one out, and then Chuck returned for another load and once more for Hub. When everything was at Chandalar, we left whatever Chuck could carry in his super-duper Super Cub with him. Then Hub and I and most of our gear flew back to Fairbanks with Dick Burley in his Cessna 180.

The flight back home was incredible. The willows and aspen dotted the hillsides with brilliant yellows, and the blueberry and cranberry bushes were vibrant red. The sky was blue, with white smoke and clouds surrounding us at times. The sweetest part of this flight was that, after over a month of camping, we were on our way home. The first thing I wanted to do was take a hot bath or two, get the dirt and grime out of my fingernails, eat a delicious T-bone steak and a ton of fresh vegetables, and sleep in a real bed with sheets and a pillow. I would miss the total silence of the wilderness, but I would also enjoy watching a little television and seeing friends again.

As we flew through the Brooks Range, we saw fires here and there, but none had been close to the Hammond River. It had been a strange air current or lack of air current containing the smoke, which brought it down our way. The entire Arctic had been shrouded in smoke for a month, but our trusty number-one bush pilot had returned and not forgotten us. When I got back home, I thought how incredibly stupid this was. No one in the world other than Chuck Gray knew our location, and if something had happened to him… well, it didn't, but I would sure as hell do it differently next time if given the chance.

CHAPTER 8
# NO MORE BEARS, PLEASE

After shooting that horrid grizzly, how I was ever talked into going hunting for brown bear is beyond me, but—willingly—I went.

Hub had once again done his detailed research and contacted a pilot named Mudhole Smith, from Cordova, to fly us to Hinchinbrook Island. I've no idea if he was the son of the famous old-time Alaskan pilot Mudhole Smith or not, but that was the name he went by, and he was one hell of an ace pilot.

We had driven from Fairbanks to Valdez where we were to meet him. When we arrived, he was already waiting for us in his Cessna 185 on floats. My first impression of him was that this was one funny little guy. He was quickly grabbing our things from the back of our pickup and loading his plane. I stood aside deciding I would just be in his way and most definitely slowing him down a notch.

During the first load, he jumped on his floats carrying a couple of boxes, and—oops—he slipped. He was a strange sight with only his stocking cap sticking out above the icy water. Not so funny were our dehydrated food packets floating away with the tide. He quickly pulled himself up onto the floats, emptied the water out of his hip boots, and grabbed a fishing net to capture our floating food. Within

a few minutes, he had scrambled into his plane and quickly emerged
wearing dry clothes. He went back to hauling boxes from our pickup
to his floats, but this time he walked a bit more carefully. After his
comical actions, we were finally ready to fly off with our crazy pilot.

With young Mudhole's 185 at warp speed and full throttle, he
made a banking quick turn over the bay of Valdez. Valdez itself is
postcard picturesque and looks like a little village in the Swiss Alps.
Immediately after leaving the bay, we were flying over the tops of
towering mountains and towards the spectacular Prince William
Sound. Looking down on this enormous ice field, the blue and green
and even brighter intense blue colors of the ice field surprised me.

At one point, we were flying so low, I could see the deep crevices
in the glacier. At the edge of the glacier, where it met the ocean,
there were giant icebergs floating offshore. It was an incredible
flight, and Mudhole had fun showing off his flying skills. We
cruised slowly around Hinchinbrook Island until he and Hub agreed
on a good spot for bear and a prime location for our camp. After
being bounced around by strong air pockets for twenty minutes, he
made a gentle landing. This time, he was a little slower with the
unpacking of our gear and much more cautious walking on the
floats, with no further mishaps.

We had planned to spend ten days on Hinchinbrook Island, but if
Mudhole happened to be in the area, he would check on us earlier.
We set up our camp on a little knoll overlooking the bay and then
hiked the beach for what was left of the day. We chose a lovely spot
where the beach was covered in clam shells. I was already drooling
over the thought of a clambake for dinner. However, when the tide
went out, we never found a single live clam. We did see a couple of
tiny little Sitka deer, and overhead several eagles were catching air
currents and were visible all afternoon. It was a lovely day of quiet
leisure.

That night, it began to rain. Correction, it began to rain not cats
and dogs, but more like tigers and wolves. Our lovely campsite
turned into a quagmire. For five days and nights it rained harder than
I've ever seen it rain. Even in the jungles of South America it never
rained that hard for so many days. With rain pouring down, there

was nothing we could do except sit in the tent, read, play cards, and bitch about the weather.

At that stage of our camping experience, we had at least upgraded from sleeping on the ground to having relatively comfortable cots. However, our tent was still so small only one person could be out of bed at a time. During this soggy dismal time, we had been cooking, eating, sleeping, and even peeing in a can, inside the tent. We were both a little cranky, and we certainly had a severe case of tent fever.

Finally, the rain reduced to a drizzle, and we ventured outside the tent before we got bedsores. The lack of a downpour was extremely welcome. I wasn't thinking about bear hunting and felt sure they too had to be holed up after all this rain. I was just happy to walk along the beach and see the beauty of the island. We got lucky, and the sun came out, so we kept walking.

We found a lovely little cove in which to sit and have our lunch, and we were given a fantastic treat by Mother Nature. There, directly in front of us, swam four sea otters. They ate, played, and entertained us. One of the otters had a baby lying on her tummy. She would rub, pat her baby, and coo in a soothing noise just like I would do to my daughter when I wanted her to take a nap. She wrapped her paws around the baby, rolled over and soon reappeared, looking as if she had given it a bath. She then seemed to be grooming it or scratching an itchy spot.

One of the other otters spent the afternoon eating. This delightful little guy would dive down, get a clam and a rock in its paws, and then, lying on its back, it would crack the clam open on the rock. At times, it would share a clam with another otter. I think even they were enjoying the sunshine, as they spent most of their time resting on their backs with their little front paws on their chests, looking like they were in church and saying a long prayer. At other times, they would look as if they were holding hands with a loved one. These darling little critters made the rainy days disappear from memory and filled my heart with utter joy.

We had hiked a few miles and then sat and watched our entertainment for perhaps two or three hours. Not being aware of the ocean and its tides, we discovered it was impossible to access where we had previously walked along the beach. What had earlier been an enjoyable hike had turned into a life-threatening climb and jump event. We had to climb a small mountain over rocky cliffs. I didn't object to the rock climbing, but when we got to one spot where the ocean was spraying over the rocks, I became hesitant.

Hub was on the cliff ahead of me. I watched as he jumped with ease across the rock ledge with the ocean waves lapping at his feet. The thought of doing the same made me want to pass out. It looked more than scary to me. It looked like my worst nightmare. Hub was yelling at me to hurry and jump, and all I could do was shake my head. I hate water, and the added noise of waves crashing against the cliff, spraying water on my face, was too much for me. This cliff placed a deathlike grip of fear on me. I could barely hang on to the cliff, let alone jump across to another ledge. At that moment, I hated this man. I hated stupid bear hunting. Most of all, I hated the frigging ocean and my fear. I yelled, screamed, and cussed, telling him, "I can't do it. I'm going back. I'll stay over here and freeze before I jump into the ocean and be slammed against those rocks."

We had an extreme intense and vulgar discussion about my refusal to jump. Hub, not so nicely told me, "Quit your whining, and just jump, or stay there and be eaten by a bear." Then he started to walk away, but he had a few departing words left in him. "God damn it. Either jump now, or I'm leaving you, because the waves are getting bigger than ever, and soon you won't be able to get across. I'm not coming back tomorrow to see your dead bear-eaten body. Donna, you have to jump as far and as high as you can. God damn it, jump, now!"

I didn't think either jumping or being eaten alive sounded particularly good at that moment. My heart was pounding so hard, my brain hurt. The waves were hitting harder at my feet, and my knees were getting weak. I called him every dirty name I knew, closed my eyes, and jumped. I landed safely at his feet. He grabbed my hand, and we scrambled farther away from the pounding ocean. It's strange how anger and fear can mess with your head, but I believe that day my anger made that jump possible.

Thankfully, we had been smart enough to pitch our tent higher than the tide line, and our tent was safe and hadn't been washed away. That little tent, as small as it was, felt like heaven to me that afternoon. I cooked the most delicious dinner of beanie-weenies (which I normally dislike), enjoyed a shot of our medicinal whiskey (which I don't like either), played the best card game ever played, and slept in the nicest sleeping bag ever made. I was so happy to be alive, not floating in the ocean, and not to have been eaten by a bear.

The following day I didn't have to worry about hanging from cliffs, being pounded to death by the surf, or eaten by a bear. It was pouring again, and the wind was blowing so hard, we were lucky to keep the tent staked down. This horrid, wet, miserable weather lasted for two more days. We had no idea if our pilot would be able to come that day or not, but we were ready if he showed up. The weather didn't stop Mudhole, and he arrived on the tenth day as planned. He was certainly a man of his word and an incredibly daring pilot indeed.

Hub had decided he needed to stay longer to find that elusive bear. He and Mudhole thought if we moved camp, the weather might be a little better on the other side of the island, and perhaps there would be more bear.

Packing wet gear is not a pleasant way to move camp. What gear had been dry was at best damp, and everything looked pretty grubby. The new location was a new location, the weather was better than before, but still our tent and bedding felt over-used, and home sounded pretty good to me. Hub, however, was determined to give it another five days because we hadn't been out of our tent except for one day and hadn't seen even a sign of a bear.

This area was decidedly different from the other camping spot or what little we had seen of it. The trees were bigger, and the undergrowth was like a slight jungle. A bear could have been hiding anywhere. It made for the possibilities of a bear being anywhere. This may have excited Hub, but remembering what it took to bring down a barren-ground grizzly, I wasn't overly thrilled. I much preferred the rivers filled with salmon and the fun of snagging them.

The salmon were spawning, and during this cycle they no longer ate, so they wouldn't take a lure, but it was still a good fight to snag one and then release it. These salmon were completing their lives' journeys from the ocean to the river where they had hatched. When they end their journeys home, perhaps traveling across a thousand miles to return to the river where they began their lives, their bodies start to deteriorate. Within a few days after spawning, they die, and the cycle begins again as their eggs are fertilized and babies are hatched.

The salmon in these rivers were too rotten to eat because they were on the last leg of their journey home. However, that was what the bear preferred, and it was why we were there. Brown bears love fishing for salmon as much as I do.

I think we did get quite lucky, and we didn't even see one nasty, old, smelly brown bear. We saw lots of eagles, a few deer, and thousands of bright red salmon on their last journey to die on the banks of the rivers and provide food for eagles and brown bears.

Mudhole returned as scheduled and gave us another low fly over the glorious Prince William Sound, dropping us back in Valdez. Oh yes, this was much more to my liking than hunting for bear. We were going fishing!

We had trailed our little boat to Valdez, so it was a straightforward matter of changing from guns to fishing rods, jumping in the boat and firing the motor. It was reported that a good run of silvers were in the bay, and I was ready for them. I would rather fish than hunt bear any day, and I would rather fish for Coho than any other salmon. They never nibble. When they hit your bait, you know it's been hit. They hit hard and then make a run to steal their meal. The best part of fishing for silvers is you always have to be ready. If you miss the hit, they're gone.

The report was correct. The silvers were in the bay and so were lots of boats. It was easy to see where the hot fishing spots were because that was where a group of boats were. I love to catch fish, but I much prefer to have some space, so we went a little farther out into the bay. I don't know how anyone on those boats did that day, but I will brag and say we limited out pretty darn fast. I'm quite sure that the other boats knew when I had caught a fish because, as anyone who has ever fished with me knows, I whoop and holler when I even get a hit and a miss.

While we were busy fishing, we heard someone yelling, and we noticed a couple of people in a little rubber life raft farther out in the bay. Strangely, the raft was moving quite fast, but we didn't hear a motor. As we got closer to the boat, we could hear them yelling for help, but the boat was still moving away from us. When we pulled up to them, they yelled that they had hooked a shark and didn't have anything to cut their line. But, much worse, they didn't want to lose their dad's fishing rod. That shark had towed them almost a mile out of the bay, and these two kids were darn scared. They were from Valdez and knew that if they went much farther out, they would be out of the bay and into much rougher water. We cut their line and towed them and their little yellow life raft back to Valdez. We also promised not to tell anyone, because their dad would have killed them or at least, never let them go out alone again with his rubber raft.

After a few days of fantastic fishing, we were on the road again heading back to Fairbanks. Fishing had been great, and it had put a smile back on my face. I thought the bear hunting was quite successful. We didn't have to trudge through heavy brush nervously wondering when an enormous brown bear would rise up and threaten us as the barren ground grizzly had. I truly had no desire to ever again hunt bear or be hunted by a bear. The rock climbing and the ocean lapping at my life had been as close to a chilling, death-defying act as I ever wanted to experience. But, we had survived.

Stopping for gas at the edge of Valdez, we heard there was a huge run of sockeyes reported at Chitna. What could be more exciting than dip-netting on the Copper River, at Chitna? We didn't have our dip-nets with us but quickly bought two, purchased a couple more coolers filled with ice, a six-pack or two of beer, and hurried out. If you're from the Pacific Northwest, you've heard of the famous Copper River salmon. That was what we were excited about. This is the best-tasting salmon in the world, and one of the strangest fishing techniques there is.

Dip-netting on the Copper River is one crazy experience, and the first time you see it, you think those people are absolutely nuts. This is a huge, fast-moving, dirty, glacier-fed, dangerous river. Yet, there are people standing up to their waist in this torrent, holding long-handled nets, looking quite silly. You have to think: what are the chances of anyone netting a fish in this vast river? But it happens.

To have a successful trip, you first need a big long-handled dip-net. The handle alone is usually about ten feet in length with a huge landing net at the end. You either stand on a rock with your net braced at the bottom of the river, waiting for a fish to hit it, or wade out into the swift river praying not to be swept away. At times, there are so many people lining the river, you need to fight for a decent spot. It may look impossible, but it's amazing how many salmon are dipped out on a good day.

Having been there several times before, we had our favorite spot to camp. Being the middle of the week, we hoped a campsite at O'Brien Creek would be open. Not only was it my preferred spot to camp, but it was also a short walk to my secret dipping hole. Not far from camp was a small rock overhang hidden by sticker bushes. Those bushes aren't any problem because for dip-netting you usually have on a heavy jacket, a raincoat, and hip boots.

Plowing ahead of Hub, I quickly got my net in the water, and there I stood bracing my big net with my hip until my arms ached. Of course, there's always a slight break to reach down for a sip of beer or to light a cigarette. Yes, that was when the first fish hit my net, and I missed it. Luck was on our side, as it then ended up in Hub's net; or maybe it was another fish, but we had one.

Hauling an eight-pound flopping fish on the end of a long-handled net is not an easy task without hitting the person next to you. Not being too concerned about that, Hub's fish smacked me in the face. Then he was yelling for me to grab the end of the net and contain the fish before it flopped back into the water. So being a good fisherman, I pounced on it and captured the first fish.

Quick as a wink, my net was back in the water, and I was determined not to take another sip of beer until I landed my very own fish. Bump, bump, and I quickly lifted my net, but no fish, so back in it went, and I braced myself again. Bump, and yes, this time I had one. Hub also had one at the same time.

This is when a person should have a video camera, but back then no one had even heard of them. Picture this: two people standing on a six- or seven-foot rock ledge, with two long-handled nets full of fish, trying to both get their fish up on the rock without knocking the other person into the water. It was what people from Montana would call a 'goat roping,' otherwise known as a crazy mess. We both had a fish, a long-handled pole, and a net hitting us, and the flying fish were whacking us. Finally, we had them on the rock, and they were trying their damndest to escape. We quickly pounced on our fish and became the winners of this contest of fish vs. man.

The biggest problem was the rock was so slippery with fish slime, it was almost impossible to stand. We decided it was time to get our treasures on ice, and we hoped the sun would dry the fish goo from the rock before we returned to try our luck again later in the day.

One of the sweetest things about fishing and camping at Chitna is returning to camp with your prize, and everyone is as happy for you as you are. The campfire at night is filled with laughter and great fish stories. There are children playing, roasting marshmallows, and making memories, alongside whiskey-drinking men and women telling wonderful Alaskan stories. The other special part of fishing at Chitna is that it's always summer when the salmon run is on, and summer means almost twenty-four hours of daylight, which leads to a round-the-clock adventure.

Returning to our rock later that day, we were lucky enough to take home ten incredibly delicious sockeye from the Copper River. I challenge anyone to have more fun fishing than can be had dip-netting for salmon. Okay, maybe snagging salmon on the Kenai River is a close runner-up, but Chitna is an experience not for the weak-armed or the serious fisherman, and it's only for crazy Alaskan residents. It's the best laugh and get-lucky fishing adventure you can imagine, and non-residents are not allowed the pleasure.

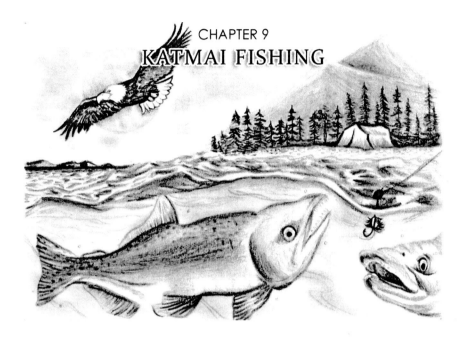

## CHAPTER 9
# KATMAI FISHING

To fish the Katmai was the dream trip of my lifetime. I had collected every piece of information I could find. I even framed the popular photo of the brown bears catching fish in the falls of the famous Brooks River. I saved my tips for months from work. Hub kicked in a nice share of the price, and I happily made reservations.

I decided to save a little money and take the train to Anchorage instead of flying from Fairbanks to the Katmai camp. The trip took about twelve hours through the most spectacular country in the world. Sitting in the lounge car drinking a beer, visiting with tourists and old-timers, and looking out at Mount Denali, was an impressive beginning. However, the best was still to come.

After spending the night in Anchorage, I caught my flight to King Salmon on Wien Air. King Salmon was at that time a small village with little to see or do. I anxiously waited for someone to tell me where to go to get my flight to the Brooks Camp. It seemed I would have to wait until the floatplane returned because the pilot was out fishing with his family instead of working. Not knowing what else to do, I found a dry spot out of the rain and sat to wait it out for as long as it took. Shortly, I heard the buzz of a plane and watched as it landed, happy to see it was a floatplane. Hopefully, it was mine.

A man who looked more like a fisherman than a commercial pilot asked, "Would you happen to want to fly somewhere today?" Oh yes, this was my pilot to the Katmai. We grabbed my duffle bag, fly rod, spinning rod and reel, and jumped into his 180 Cessna on floats. Being so excited, I couldn't sit still. I think I talked his ear off about fishing. He told me he had taken his wife and son out to where the salmon were supposed to be running for the day, and after he dropped me off, he would go back to fishing with his family.

He gave me a nice little tour over the lake and the river where I planned to fish. He was happy, as that day the lake was calm and made for an easy landing, but he told me it wasn't always this easy. He warned me, "This is one crazy lake. When the wind blows, it can bring in tons of floating pumice from the volcano, and sometimes you can't even land anywhere close to camp. You should know that you may not get out on the day you planned. I think you have reservations to be picked up in five days. I'll be here around noon or later, weather permitting. You'll have to listen for me and be sure to check with the lodge about my schedule. Have a good trip, and leave some fish for others to catch." He jumped back in his plane and flew off to enjoy of a day of fishing with his family.

As he departed, I picked up my gear and started up the trail to where I thought I should go. Down the beach, not more than fifty yards from me, stood a big old brown bear. He didn't seem to care about me, so I eased my way up the trail to the first building I saw. Luckily, it was where I was supposed to check in. It was a cute little store with a desk for registering, and a young boy gave me my key and told me to come back when I was ready, and he would tell me about where and how to fish. So off I went to find my cabin.

Cabin #7 was mine, and all I cared about was dropping off my duffel bag and getting out to the river. I gave the cabin a quick look, and I will say it was just like it should have been. It was a cute little cabin hidden in the trees, containing nothing more than the essentials. I dug around until I found my mosquito repellent, my spinning rod and reel, and hurried back to the little store.

The young man in charge that afternoon was a fount of fishing information. He asked what sort of gear I had and then checked all the lures, flies, and junk I had brought with me. Smiling a little, he suggested I might not want to use any of it. Hoping he wasn't selling me a bill of goods, I bought the gigantic, vividly colored flies he recommended. Next, he gave me a map and some advice about the bears in that area. He asked if I wanted a guide and then laughed and told me, "You won't need one because Pete is here, and he loves blonde-haired women who like to fish. He'll show you the way to the river and the best spots to fish."

He was right: Pete did show me where to fish, where to cross the river, and gave me instructions to be very loud when I was going through the trees, so as not to surprise a bear. Before we got to his favorite spot, we had to walk along the path through a tight closed area of small trees and brush. Pete was talking loudly and warned me that this area was where I needed to be careful. If I was alone I had to make a lot of noise, and singing and whistling seemed to be a good bear repellent. When we came to the river, which was flowing pretty high that day, he showed me a safe spot to cross and warned me that if it started to rain heavily to hurry back across before it got too high, or I would have to spend the night alone with the bears.

After crossing the river, it was just a short trip up the trail, and we were at the famous Brooks Falls; yes, the one in all the pictures with the brown bears grabbing the salmon. That afternoon, there were no fishing bears, and so we sat while Pete attached his favorite fly to my line. It was larger and much more colorful than I was used to using, but never question a local fisherman because they do know what works best. Pete was right: I cast his strange fly, and *wham*—on the first cast I had a lovely salmon. It was all picture-perfect and a dream come true with the salmon jumping on the end of my line, the falls in the background, and no bear around for the moment.

Pete became bored with my cast after cast of excitement and gave me his best advice to keep going up river because the bears would be arriving to eat soon. Right, he was, for as he departed, two big brown bears arrived, and I left after a few minutes of watching the experts grab a fish with their massive paws, shove it into their giant mouths, and immediately grab more. At that moment I wished I had a camera, but no, I didn't. I was a fisherman, not a photographer. Notice I say fisherman because back then we didn't recognize the term *fisherwoman*.

Wandering upriver to see what the water farther on looked like, I met another fisherman, and he had a large king salmon on his line. He yelled, "Do you have a net?" No, I didn't because I intended to release everything I caught. I watched him fight his mighty salmon for fifteen or twenty minutes, while I caught and released three beauties of my own. It was getting near dusk, and I knew we needed to get back before dark. I hollered to him that I was leaving, and maybe he should think about horsing that one in with the hope of either getting it ashore or breaking his line. He yelled back to me, "No way. Could you send someone back with a flashlight? Tell them I have a record-breaking fish on, and I've been fighting it for over forty-five minutes, and I'm not quitting until I get him landed." As I left, I hoped he didn't run into any bears in the dark, and I hurried noisily back to camp singing as loudly as possible to warn any bears of my approach.

When this man still hadn't returned after dinner was finished, a couple of the guides went in search of him. The other two fishermen—both doctors—and I sat around a small campfire, talking fishing, and waited for their return. In the distance, we saw a flare shoot into the sky, and all the employees in camp went racing out. Not having any idea what it meant, we were all a little concerned that it wasn't a good sign.

A short time later, the guides returned with the man on a stretcher, and the doctors immediately jumped to service. They were sure he had suffered a minor heart attack but was out of danger. The only thing the man seemed to care about was if they had brought his fish with him. Sadly, it wasn't quite a record king salmon, but I'm sure it was one fish that man will never forget. The doctors and I ended the night with a rousing game of poker, with them winning all my matchsticks, and they proclaimed me the loser but the best beer drinker in the camp.

The next day I switched to fishing for rainbow trout, and it was an incredible day. I can't say I caught as many rainbows as I had salmon, but the ones I hooked were big, bold, and beautiful. The river was crystal clear and demanded that my fly land gently so as not to disturb these beauties. After a few rather sloppy casts, my arm loosened up and I improved, but still this water made for difficult fishing. I think the magic of fly-fishing is not what you hook, but how well you present the fly. That's the story I told the doctors later that night when they asked how my day was, and they teased me about my fly- fishing philosophy for days.

After a few more days out fishing for salmon with the bears, my fingers were becoming callused, my casting arm was stiff, and my heart was happy. Every day, we had all been well fed with hearty breakfasts of eggs, bacon or ham, hash browns, and pancakes. Lunch was a huge box packed with a ham sandwich, deviled eggs, some fresh fruit, and a beer if you had brought it with you. The doctors were good enough to share theirs with me, as I hadn't brought any. Oh, but dinner was what no one wanted to miss. It covered the table with fresh salmon caught that day, potatoes, vegetable, salads, and several pies. It was a spread for royalty and hungry fishermen.

Each night the doctors, heart-attack man, the cooks, guides, and I would play poker until the wee hours. The doctors had an abundance of whiskey with them, so late at night it became more a game of the losers of each hand having to slam a shot of whiskey. The poker game then would turn into a silly game of Indian, and roaring laughter with fun was had by one and all.

Sadly, too soon, it was time to pack up my gear and catch my flight to King Salmon, and then on to Anchorage for my train trip back to Fairbanks.

As I sat on the train from Anchorage to Fairbanks, happily recalling my fantastic fishing trip, we stopped at Denali State Park for a short break. Not paying attention to anything except the breathtaking scenery, I was surprised by a tap on the shoulder and found two good friends standing behind me with huge smiles on their faces. They knew I had been to the Katmai fishing, and at first I thought they were waiting to hear about my latest fishing trip.

After a few minutes of hugs and welcomes, I could tell they had something else urgent to say. Finally, they burst out with, "Isn't this a day to remember?" My silly reply was, "Well, it's a good day but not as good as the week of fishing I've just had." I could tell from their expressions this wasn't quite the appropriate reply. Still smiling, they said, "You haven't heard that the eagle has landed."

I knew my face was telling them I had no idea what they were talking about. Being extremely excited, they were both talking at once, and I finally understood what was going on. This was a day in history: July 20, 1969—the day Neil Armstrong walked on the moon. Their exciting tale sort of took the cherry off my fishing stories, but I would remember both. The eagle had landed. *'One small step for man, one giant leap for mankind.'* And I had also completed my lifelong dream of fishing the Katmai.

CHAPTER 10
# FISHING LOVE STORIES

Salmon are king of all fish in Alaska, and I've enjoyed each and every one I've ever caught, but I won't forget any of the other incredible local fish either.

Oh, those majestic Arctic graylings with their vibrant iridescent colors are such a delightful northern fish and not found any longer in many of the lower forty-eight states. These beauties are a fly-fishermen's joy and abundant in Alaska. They will always have a spot in my fishing heart for the fun they have brought me.

Then there's the fighting, kick-butt northern pike with his or her gnarly teeth waiting to shred your hand when you release them from your favorite lure. As soon as the ice was off the lakes, rivers, or sloughs around Fairbanks, we were always ready for a fly-in to catch the action.

This late spring or early summer fly-in to Lake Minchuminia was something I looked forward to throughout the winter, and it was never a disappointment. It was a yearly tradition for a group of our pilot friends to get together for a day of fishing at this special lake in the Alaskan Range. This group of men, women, and at times a couple of kids, came prepared to do some serious fishing. The northern pike from this lake were bigger than average and the most flavorful, and we all wanted to take a few home for summer barbeques.

As soon as the planes landed, people were busy hooking up their favorite lure. It quickly became a fierce competition of the biggest and the most fish caught in one hour. Then there were the arguments of which lure was the best, at least for that particular day. My favorite was always a red-and-white daredevil, and I would stick with it no matter what others were using because I was positive I caught larger fish with it.

The thrilling thing about pike is, when they hit your lure, they could almost knock your rod out of your hand. After the initial hit, they don't compare to the fight of a silver salmon, but they still give a good fight to escape. Once you land it, your treacherous work begins.

Pike teeth are so numerous and needle-sharp, a special metal line is needed to connect to the lure because their teeth will simply cut a normal monofilament line. To remove the lure, a pair of leather gloves and needle-nose pliers are a necessity, or your hands will be shredded to bits. Even with this bit of difficulty, I still find it fun to hold that slippery squirming fish and try to release it without ending up with a sharp hook in my hand or a mangled glove from those gnarly teeth.

During our fishing contests, someone usually took time out to build a fire and threw one of the pike on for a tasty treat. The great thing about these people was they always came prepared to fish, cook, and would add a generous splash of Bailey's Irish Cream to any hot chocolate sitting around. It made for quite an incredible day of fishing, eating, laughing, and looking at one of the most spectacular mountains in the world. We had a picture-window view of Denali (Mount McKinley) in all her wondrous glory as she rose 20,156 feet into the air. From the lake, she appeared in the distance as an incredible shade of blue but mostly covered in white from snow or glaciers, and in the foreground were fields of wild flowers. It was hard to turn one's back on this glorious sight and pay attention to fishing, but we did.

Our group was super lucky that day, and we all went home with enough fresh pike to satisfy our appetites with a few extras added for summer parties. On the way back to Fairbanks, we hit some serious turbulent air, throwing the plane this way and that for several minutes. This group of pilots weren't new to flying, and they were all considered to be fine bush pilots. No one was too concerned about the turbulence, except a few passengers had some rough moments with airsickness.

As the summer progressed, Hub and I would load our boat and hit the Yukon River or Minto Flats for more pike fishing. I was always a little uncomfortable on the Yukon, as it seemed to me to be one rather scary, huge, grey piece of water, plus I was never very lucky on it. I much preferred Minto Flats, as it was more exciting boating through dozens of connecting sloughs, and each one looking perfect for pike.

On one of those trips to the Flats, we spent several days exploring the different sloughs, fishing in many or just enjoying life on the water. We found a little old abandoned cabin and used it for our base camp. As the rain poured down, this little cabin was highly appreciated, but rain or no rain, we were out on the water six or eight hours a day. One of the most active spots for pike happened to be right around the bend from our cabin, so it was easy to take a break and return for lunch or a short nap.

After one of those naps, we returned to the hot fishing spot near our cabin. I decided to be adventuresome and started playing with different lures to see what worked and what the fish rejected. Hub chose the old reliable red-and-white daredevil, while I foolishly chose a new—highly recommended by the local fishermen—ugly yellow-striped lure. After one cast, Hub's line went zinging. Thirty minutes later, he was still trying to bring his fish to the boat. After finally getting a look at this monster, he became a little more nervous. We foolishly hadn't brought a net with us. It hadn't seemed necessary at the time because, so what if we lost a fish or two? We planned to release most of them anyway. However, this one was too huge not to care about, and we seriously wanted him in our boat.

Fishing these sloughs wasn't like being in a lake with gravel bottoms. There were reeds, willows, fallen trees, and other things for a fish to tangle your line in. Hub was doing his best to tire out this lunker and yet keep him away from any of the thousands of obstacles. He finally got him up to the boat, and we were dragging him to open water when another boat arrived. These fishermen could see the size of this beauty and understood our problem. One of the men had his net ready and took a swipe at Hub's fish. Oops, he missed, and then he nearly lost his net. Thankfully, Mr. Pike was too tired to care, and the second swoop of the net had him captured and quickly thrown over into our boat.

The gentlemen with the net were almost as happy as we were, and we rewarded them with a cold beer for their rescue. Hub generously revealed what lure he had used to hook this beauty, and then we all attached the magic daredevil and continued fishing.

When we returned home, the first thing we did was have this monster weighed. It registered in at twenty-four pounds fourteen ounces by the Fish and Game and was the largest pike caught in the Minto Flats for several years. And we came close to losing it.

We returned to this hot spot many times that summer, but so did the men with the net and many of their friends. This is one good reason never to tell anyone where your gold is buried, or where your favorite fishing spot is.

CHAPTER 11
# FISHING, A BABY, AND A CARIBOU HUNT

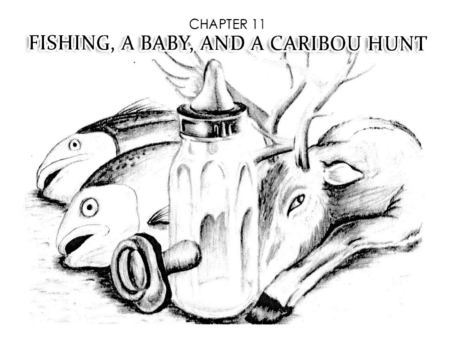

In 1867, William Seward purchased Alaska from Russia for two cents an acre for a total of seven million dollars. They called it Seward's Folly or Seward's Icebox.

One hundred and two years later, Seward was to become our home. Moving from the freezing north of Fairbanks to Seward was my fishing dream come true. I was happy to think I could throw away my parka and mukluks and replace them with rain gear and fishing boots. Little did I know how cold the icy winds blowing off Resurrection Bay and the nearby glaciers could be. I don't think I've ever been as frozen as when the temperature was hovering around thirty above zero, with the wind blowing and the rain flowing. This combination computed to a wind chill of minus fourteen. I was glad to have kept my parka and mukluks.

The worst thing about Seward's rain and cold was the ice. It would become so icy that the locals wore cleats on their shoes to prevent them from falling. One local woman wore heavy wool socks over her shoes so she could navigate the slippery streets, which may have seemed funny when I first saw her, but later I thought how brilliant she was. On one short drive to our home during an extremely icy period, as we slowly tried to negotiate a slight curve on the gravel road, we had to stop because there were three vehicles slip-sliding in front of us. Two went into the ditch, with the third smashing into both. As we tried to avoid the mishap in front of us, our pickup slowly slid forward into the ditch, too. With nothing left to do, we tried to walk home without cleats on our boot and ended up falling, crawling, and cussing our way home.

The other downside of Seward's weather was what they called summer. It rained, rained and rained. Being a gardener, I planted my little garden at the end of May, hoping for warm weather. By the end of June, I had mold growing on all the leaves, and the plants were still dwarfed. By July, I had a few sprigs of lettuce that were decent, but I will admit my garden was just one wet, soggy disaster that first year. I had been spoiled by Fairbank's warm, sunny twenty-four hours of sunlight, which were a gardener's dream.

Giving up on my gardening was easy because it meant I could fish every day. I would drive for a mile, walk about another mile, then drop my line off an old transport pier, and fish to my heart's content. Normally, I would catch some sort of strange-looking fish to entertain me, even though it might not have been a fish I would have chosen to eat. At times, I caught nothing but Irish Lords. They were ugly fish with a slightly poisonous spine, so it took a little care to release them from my hook, but it was still fun. On the weekends, I was often joined by an old couple from Anchorage, who were experts at catching flounder, and they taught me a few secret fishing tricks. This fun-loving couple loved to fish as much as I did, and we would share our favorite fishing or hunting stories, coffee, lunch, and the catch of the day. Who could ask for more, except perhaps for a boat?

We decided we actually needed a boat to properly fish the waters of Resurrection Bay. It wasn't what you would call a beauty, by any means, and needed a lot of work, but the price was right. We quickly started sanding the fiberglass bow and refinishing the woodwork. After many hours of dirty hard work, it was ready for a paint job. Painting was the only thing we hired out, and the shop did a meticulous job of making our boat presentable. Once we acquired a proper motor, we were out on the water almost daily, weather permitting.

It wasn't a large boat, so we usually fished inside the bay around Thumbs Cove or to the edge of Fox Island. The wonderful thing about Resurrection Bay was when the salmon were in, you could hang close to shore, not venturing too far out but still have fantastic fishing. So our little boat worked pretty well for us ocean novices.

One of the reasons we didn't take a chance on rough water was because I was eight months pregnant. However, my love of fishing wasn't going to keep me onshore.

The morning of August 9 was spectacular with the bay as flat as glass. At the dock, everyone was excited, as the salmon were in the bay, and people were getting lucky. So off we went and headed across the bay to Thumbs Cove, where it was reported the silvers were hitting like crazy. Trolling for only a few minutes, *wham*, Hub had hooked a beauty, and it was fighting like crazy. A few minutes later, I got lucky, too.

Like a nutty woman, I was whooping, hollering, and laughing. Hooking a good fighting fish to me is the best fun there is. We were laughing, getting our lines tangled, stopping to get the wild flopping fish in the hold, more laughing, and then finally getting the lines back in the water. It was hit after hit with several misses for about thirty minutes. Then our lively action came to an abrupt halt. No one in any of the other boats seemed to be getting hits either, and most of the boats were leaving for a better spot—hopefully. We followed suit and headed towards Humpy Cove, hoping to limit out for the day, the limit being six salmon per person per day, and we had a couple more to go to fill the freezer and the smoker for the winter.

Around the bend from Humpy Cove, the wind picked up, and dark clouds appeared, so we decided to turn back towards home. It was about 3:00 p.m., and the water usually got a little rough about that time, but this storm was coming in super fast. Hanging close to shore, the water wasn't too rough, but we still had to cross the bay. We could see the waves were kicking up some seriously big whitecaps.

Hub was a good captain and knew how to hit the waves, but they were still severely pounding my insides. I was a happy woman to finally reach the harbor and be standing on dock, slightly wet but safe. As we were loading the fish into the truck, Hub said, "You're looking a little funny. How do you feel?" Then he started to comment on my strange new way of walking. That is *not* what you ever want to tell a pregnant woman. I threw my fish in the cooler, slammed the door, and glared at him for the ride home.

Once we were home, I had to admit to him that I felt pretty crappy. As I had a few sharp pains, I took out my Dr. Spock book to see what could be wrong and what the good doctor recommended. Doc Spock advised the best thing for false labor was to walk, so up and down our road I walked.

Seward had two doctors at that time. Doc Watson was our neighbor, and when he saw me traipsing back and forth in front of his house, he called Dr. John to be prepared for an early baby delivery. On my next pass by his house, he came outside and sternly told me to get to the hospital. The morning of August 10, I delivered a four-pound-four-ounce baby girl. She was so tiny that the fish we had caught that day were twice her size.

Happily, she was healthy and perfect in every way. Everyone was happy except Dr. John; he wasn't pleased that I had been out in the boat that day. He informed me that with the boat hitting the water as hard as it did, it had knocked her right down into the birth canal. He went on and on about how I had risked my pregnancy and I should have thought twice about my fishing trip. Then I reminded him, "But you told me I could do anything I normally did, just not to take up horseback riding if I wasn't used to it." He admitted he should have given me better instructions, knowing I did such crazy things and that I wasn't a stay-at-home sort of woman.

I didn't tell him that the week before we had hiked into one of our favorite mountain lakes, which was a good hard climb, even if you weren't pregnant. When I looked back, it gave me the quivers to think what could have happened if she had decided to arrive early. I guess I would have had to be like the Indians of long ago and just squatted in the tent, while Hub went for help. Then I would have had to walk out because the lake was too small for a float plane, and I'm sure Hub couldn't have carried me all that way. It didn't happen, so for that I was thankful, and I certainly wasn't going to tell that story to Dr. John.

I did become a stay-at-home woman for several months, but then Hub asked if I wanted to go caribou hunting. That sounded so good, but we had a baby, and who would I ever leave her with? Dr. John's wife, Hope, volunteered, and feeling good about a babysitter, off we went to go hunting caribou.

We were new to that area and had spent most of our time hunting caribou out of Fairbanks, where the herds are numerous. This time, we had to drive for about four hours before we were into a country suited for hunting. We stopped at several roadhouses, hoping to catch up on the latest hunting gossip.

It wasn't sounding as if the caribou had migrated to this area as we had been told earlier. Hub decided to contact a pilot friend and made fast plans to fly out to find the herds the next morning. Sleeping in the back of the pickup in a camper shell at minus twenty degrees is never fun, but that's what we did. At around 8:00 a.m., our pilot arrived and told us it would only be a ten-minute flight to get to a nice herd. It was a quick trip, and we spotted the herd immediately. We landed slightly over the hill away from them, climbed the hill through deep snow, then lay down, and took aim. Soon we had two caribou to load into his 180 Cessna. We were back at the pickup in less than an hour. This wasn't what we would have called a normal caribou hunt; it just felt all wrong to simply fly out, find a herd, and never give the animal a chance. We decided to spend the day really hunting on foot in search of these ghostly animals. Our pilot had seen a few more scattered close by, so we could do a real hunt for them.

Driving to the summit, we spotted a small herd off in the distance with a larger herd looking as if it would be joining them. Daylight being our worst enemy, we were sure it would be too dark to be successful by the time we reached them.

The other problem was that I was getting sicker by the minute. We decided to try to find a bed for the night and then continue hunting in the morning. Luckily, just a few miles up the road, there was a hunting lodge. By the time we got there, I was burning up with fever and way too sick to sleep in the freezing camper. The lodge told us they didn't have a room, but when they saw how sick I was, they said they had two beds in a room with four other people.

Happy to have a warm bed, we took it and crashed for the night. Sometime later, I awoke to a woman screaming and throwing things around the cabin. A little nervous, I leaned over the edge of the bed trying to understand what the commotion was, and an extremely angry woman yanked the covers off me and was right in my face, yelling, "Who are you, and what the hell are you doing in our cabin?" At that point, her husband and the other couple were trying, unsuccessfully, to quiet her down. She was still throwing her stuff in a pack and screaming, "I'm not sleeping in a room with people I don't know. They could be crazy killers for all you know. I'm leaving. This lodge is going to have to find me a room alone, or I'll sue their ass."

At that point, I jumped out of bed, ran to the door, and threw up everything I had eaten that day and the week before. The screaming woman was beyond words and upset at the horrid stench from my mess on the doorstep. Then she came rushing out the door, pushed me aside, and joined me. We were both barfing, shaking from the cold, and gagging from the stench.

When both our stomachs were empty, she looked at me and said, "We're a fine mess. You look like you might be dying, and I feel like I want to die." We went back inside the cabin together. I went back to bed, and I guess she did also. I don't know why I was so sick, but I do know her illness was simply from way too much booze.

Bright and early the next morning, we quietly packed up and left our strange little cabin mate. Crossing the road not far from the cabins were perhaps seventy to a hundred caribou. I was still too sick to care about caribou, so Hub jumped out alone and quickly shoot two nice young bulls. I was just happy we were going home, but it felt good to have a supply of winter meat with some left over for the lovely people who were taking care of our daughter.

I would rate this hunt as one of the strangest caribou hunts I have ever been on: not good, not bad, but just weird.

## CHAPTER 12
# AN ALASKAN BUSH BABY

**The bush: a remote place in Alaska with no city close by, no neighbors, no stores, no electricity, no running water, a lot of nos, and a few oh my gods.**

Moving to Alaska from a rural area in Montana in 1967 wasn't a significant adjustment for me. I survived the sixty-below-zero winters in Fairbanks just fine. I had already spent a summer camping in the Brooks Range and lived to tell the tale. I had hunted caribou, moose, Dall sheep, and bear with the big boys. I had fished from the little rivers of the interior to the open ocean off Resurrection Bay, and I hadn't died yet. I was no longer a cheechako (newcomer to Alaska).

So what was the big deal about moving to a cabin in the bush? Everyone seemed to think it was one utterly ludicrous idea. Even my father wasn't happy with this move, and Dr. John was throwing a little fit. My friends simply shook their heads, and one of them said, "No way would I let my husband drag me off to a cabin in the wilderness so he could play some kind of mountain-man game. You're just plain crazy if you go with him."

I did give our plan a serious second thought when Dr. John, my friend and pediatrician, started asking some extremely sound questions. He shook his head in disgust and asked, "What will you do if Brandi gets seriously sick, or if the weather is too bad to fly, or it's so cold the airplane won't start?" He asked some other hair-raising questions, but these particular ones truly hit on the reality of what the hell we were doing.

Still, I tried to explain to my friends, my doctor—and anyone with questions—about what we were going to be doing and why. However, my answers were a little weak, since I wasn't certain what we would be doing or why, even though Hub had done an admirable job of selling this idea to me. The only thing I actually knew was that we were going to be mining gold somewhere in the Brooks Range, at a place called Linda Creek. We would be full partners with Earl Boese, who was getting too old to work alone. We would have one cabin, and Mr. Boese would have a separate cabin. I was supposed to be the cook while Hub and Boese did the mining.

Hub's sales pitch to make this move always started with, "Remember before we moved to Alaska, this was our plan—to live in the bush someday. Remember all the books we read about how Bob Marshall loved the Brooks Range and how much we loved Bob Marshall's books. Remember how we planned to homestead or mine for gold." Remembering our dream was a daily pep talk.

Yes, I did remember all those dreams, but sometimes the talking is better than the doing. I was becoming more dubious every day, especially with all the negative talk from others. Life is different for a mother with a child than for a young woman married to a man with the dream of being the next explorer of a vast wilderness. I was wavering between going and not going, still pondering if it was an adventure of a lifetime, or maybe a supremely stupid and foolish idea.

My father called me one day from Montana and gave me an earful of what he thought about this move. He wasn't a man who told people what to do, but he told me in no uncertain terms how stupid it was. That same day, I received a package from him in the mail. This little goodie box contained needles and thread inside sterile bottles, used for stitching a wound, plus more needles of all sizes. There were several vials of penicillin with needles ready for injections. He had included bandages, gauze, and lots of tape, also a small metal flask of whiskey, a huge bottle of aspirin, and various tubes of ointments. I was starting to understand how serious things could get, and then I saw a note at the bottom of the box. Inside the note was a bullet, and the note read, "In case things get too tough, use this on that crazy bastard, bundle up that precious baby, and come home."

I had a good laugh, but also took it somewhat more seriously and appreciated his concern. I knew the penicillin was sent by Uncle Tige because I had seen these vials before. He had always gotten them from Doc Hollaway, the local veterinary. Uncle Tige thought if it was good enough for an animal, it was good enough for a human. Laughing a little and looking at the penicillin, I decided it was actually quite a smart idea. If not for our personal use, it might still come in handy for the dogs. This was something I wouldn't ever have thought of, but these two old Montana cowboys knew what was needed, and so I packed it all in the box going north.

The time to depart my sweet little home on the coast of Alaska was all coming down to the wire. It was no longer just fun talk; it was quickly becoming a reality. Our cozy little house and our brave little fishing boat had already been sold. Hub had quit his job as a guidance counselor and science teacher at Seward High School. We attended going-away parties, and once you say goodbye, there's no turning back.

My friends loaded me down with art supplies of every medium, hoping to turn me into an artist. Not only did I not have the talent, but who, with a baby, cooking three meals a day, has time to do any finger painting? One dear friend gave me a journal, which I used to keep a record of our daily life at Linda Creek, not knowing that someday it would be where my memories would be stored to write this book.

Our truck was soon packed, and we went on our way to Fairbanks, the first step in this trip to our new home on Linda Creek. Returning to Fairbanks was an exciting reunion with long-standing friends, and introducing them to our ten-month-old daughter was the highlight of it all. After visiting with friends for a couple of days, Hub was getting anxious to get on with our plans. Off he went to sell

our pickup, put our personal items in storage, and make
arrangements for our flight north.

I spent the day at Lindy's Grocery, the only store at that time
making shipments to the bush. It was an incredible little store, filled
with all the food and sundry items a person living in the wilderness
would ever need. Wandering aimlessly from aisle to aisle, I must
have looked overwhelmed because Mr. Lindy, the owner, took pity
on me and asked if he could help. When I told him I was moving to
the Brooks Range, he invited me to his office. We talked for a while
about life in the bush, and then he set up an account for us. He
explained how to make an order with the store and gave me a ream
of order blanks. The order blanks had everything in his store listed
for individual or case lots. All I needed to do was check the item I
wanted, how many individuals or cases, and how it was to be sent.
He asked for a list of people that would possibly be sending or
picking up our orders, and he added their names in his notebook
under our account. He assured me that all orders would be put on
Wien Airline and sent to Wiseman, or they could be picked up by a
friend on his account list. This wonderful little store not only
delivered to individuals living in the bush, but also to all the villages
in the remote areas of Interior Alaska.

I took an hour looking over his store with my order sheet in hand.
Not having any idea what three people would eat in a month or
more, I was rather intimidated by it all. Once again, Mr. Lindy took
pity on me and gave me some suggestions on what he thought was
necessary, and then I added a few items I felt were essential. Just
trying to figure out the number of Pampers was mind-boggling to
someone used to being able to go to the store whenever something
was needed. Soon, there would be no more dropping by a store to
grab something for dinner.

I frantically started checking off cases of vegetables of every sort
and bought a large amount of bacon. Mr. Lindy recommended at
least two slabs of uncut bacon, and instructed me that no matter how
old the bacon was or even if it was moldy, it was still okay to eat;
just rinse it off with vinegar, and it would be fine. Then I checked off
one large bottle of vinegar. He then suggested I might want another

one because it was good for any infection, sore throat, cough, or upset stomach, plus it would make the laundry smell better.

My list kept growing with several jars of mayonnaise, butter, cooking oil, flour, sugar, rice, pasta, and spices, and I had only just begun my checklist. The list was long, and it was shocking to see the final price, but it was more shocking to see all this food in one location, ready to be loaded on a plane later that week.

On June 8, 1971, we left civilization behind and flew north to the Brooks Range. That morning our friends—Les and Terry—drove us to a small private airstrip where our pilots were waiting. We said a quick goodbye, and they promised to take good care of our two dogs until they could also be flown north to join us. Our friend Karl Maerzluft was my pilot, and he would be taking Brandi and me, plus all the personal goodies we could fit into his plane. Hub was flying in another plane and carrying more supplies.

I had become used to flying in small planes, and it was comforting to relax for the ninety-minute flight and chat with a friend. Leaving Fairbanks and crossing over the Yukon River was familiar, as I had done this part of the trip several times before. As we flew deeper into the Brooks, the mountains became much larger and more incredible with the hillsides bright green, the mountain tops white with snow, and the rivers and lakes an incredible blue-green.

It was a perfect flying day with little or no air turbulence, and even Brandi seemed to be enjoying the journey, sitting like a little angel looking out the window and napping occasionally. As we got closer to our destination, Karl reminded me that at least we would have a two-way radio in the cabin for communication with the outside world. It was comforting to know if anything went seriously wrong, we could contact him or perhaps others. He was a pilot for Wien Air and flew over Linda Creek daily on his scheduled flight to Nome. Again I heard the message of concern in my friend's voice, but there we were, and we kept flying north.

As we approached our new home on Linda Creek, Karl gave me a couple of low fly-bys to check it out. Before he set up for landing, he asked, "Are you sure you want to do this? We can turn around now

and go back to Fairbanks. Just say the word and I'll turn it around."
But I didn't say a word.

Viewing our new home from the little window of the plane, my
first sight below was of four log buildings: Boese's cabin, a shop
with a tractor in front, what I thought was our cabin, and another
building. Below the buildings looked like what must have been the
mining area. It all looked rather cute to me, so I gave him the nod to
go ahead and land.

Hub had already arrived, and he and Mr. Boese came to greet us.
Mr. Boese looked much younger than I thought he would. I had been
told he needed help because of his age, but he looked pretty chipper
to me. The nicest thing about him was he seemed to be particularly
interested in how Brandi enjoyed the flight, and he was all smiles
whenever he looked at her. That's a good way to a mother's heart.

After the introductions had been completed, we followed Boese
to what he said was the main cabin—or our cabin. My first
impression was, wow, this must be the nicest cabin in the Brooks
Range and one of the biggest. I have to admit I was pleasantly
surprised.

Mr. Boese quickly set about making coffee. In any camp in
Alaska, offering a cup of coffee is traditional and shows polite
manners. It's like saying, 'Welcome to my home.' The men sat down
for their coffee, while Brandi and I surveyed the cabin. It was
surprisingly clean and much more orderly than I would ever have
expected from a man living alone in the bush. I think Mr. Boese was
extremely busy getting ready for a woman's arrival.

I was shocked to find a freezer and a small propane stove. I didn't
know how a freezer was possible when there was no electricity.
When I asked about this, Boese explained, "The freezer is run by
propane, and the propane stove is to be used only for short periods of
time, like for a quick cup of coffee. Normally, you need to use the
wood stove. Today is an exception because you need time to move
in and take care of your baby. Tomorrow you can start cooking on
the wood stove, and I'll show you how to get water and how other
things around here work, but today you can use the propane. Just
make a quick dinner so you don't use too much because it's
expensive and hard to get."

That was a relief because I didn't want to start off our partnership trying to light the wood stove and smoking up the cabin on the first day. This was just the beginning of my lessons of living in the bush. Soon, I would have to learn to light a proper fire in the wood stove and cook breakfast, lunch, and dinner on that critter, but thankfully, not that day.

While the men went out to look at the mining operation, I got busy checking in every nook and cranny to see everything there. There was a small window in the corner above a double kitchen sink. It was nice to have the added light and be able to look outside while washing the dishes or bathing Brandi. Checking the freezer, I was elated to see packages of moose, caribou, and sheep meat, nicely wrapped and solidly frozen. I noticed a trapdoor in the middle of the room, and I had to see what this could be. I was a little nervous because maybe it was where Boese kept his gold, and I shouldn't have been looking there. As I lifted the trapdoor, I could see a short ladder going down, but it was too dark to see anything else. I spotted a flashlight hanging on a nail, and being a little excited and devilishly nosey, I turned it on with the thoughts of gold glimmering at the bottom. No, it was only a cellar for storing food. I was a little disappointed, but at least I knew where all the food I had bought in Fairbanks could be safely stored.

Closing the trapdoor and looking at the rest of the house, I could see there were lots of Blazo boxes around the cabin. These boxes are the normal kitchen cabinets in many Alaskan cabins. They're the wooden crates in which white gas, kerosene, or aviation gas are packed, and make perfect stools, cabinets, and if worse comes to worst, you can burn them.

These boxes made up the cabinets for storing our pots, pans, and cooking supplies, and in the bedroom area, they were where we stored our clothes. There was one store-bought little dresser dividing the kitchen/living area from our bedroom. I thought this would be the ideal spot for Brandi's toys.

The most modern item in the kitchen was a nice, relatively new dining set. The table was topped with 1960s green Formica (a collector's item today), and the chairs were covered in red vinyl. The most unusual thing about our cabin was that someone had put up wallpaper of incredibly bright yellow and red flowers, and this paper covered every wall and cabinet. It was so wild, it made my eyes cross for the first few days, but eventually, I hardly noticed this strange artistic endeavor.

It didn't take long to explore the bedroom, as there was only a double bed, a few Blazo boxes, and a back door. I was glad to see there were two doors in case of fire. Off to the side of the bedroom were a tiny boxed-in closet and a small rollaway bed.

Bed! Oh my god, we had no crib for Brandi. What could we have been thinking? What in the world were we going to do, and where could my little girl sleep? It made me worry about what other day-to-day things we had overlooked in our buying and packing. As soon as Hub returned, I filled his ears with what rotten parents we were and what a bed dilemma we had to face.

The next morning, bright and early, we were out cutting small spruce trees, peeling the bark off, and making a crib. In the cache (an Alaskan storage area, usually built on stilts, to keep the varmints out), Hub found a sheet of plywood for the bottom, and I had a piece of foam rubber which we used as a mattress. For some strange reason, I had also brought a huge amount of fabric with me, and I quickly started sewing a cover for the foam pad. It certainly wasn't what you could buy at Sears, but it looked and felt pretty safe and sturdy. Best of all, it was ready for Brandi at nap time, and she seemed to be happy enough with it.

I do remember the first evening in the cabin quite well because I worried what Boese would think of cold ham sandwiches made with store-bought bread. I had made a whole loaf of them before we left Fairbanks, along with a huge batch of brownies, and that's what I served. Other than his smiling at Brandi, he was pretty quiet, but he did tell me, "You didn't even use any propane for dinner, and those sandwiches were just like eating at a restaurant." I guess that was good because he thanked me for dinner and again thanked me for not using any propane. After he left, Hub and I had a little laugh and agreed that the propane probably was a cherished item, only to be used when absolutely necessary.

At 5:00 a.m. the next morning Hub was up, lighting the wood stove for me to cook breakfast. Thank you, Hub, as I would have taken way too long to get the fire going, and I would rather practice the fire on my own without anyone's watchful eyes. I made oatmeal because I had found a huge supply in the cabinet and thought Boese must like it. I also made pan toast and fried a few pieces of bacon. It was nice to know that both Boese and Brandi liked the oatmeal, so that was one hurdle crossed.

Hub may have been there to light the morning fire, but then I was on my own. In the past, I had started many campfires, but never one in a cooking stove. A couple of hours before lunch, I did my fire practice. I started as I would to make a campfire; first, I crumpled up some wads of paper, then some small kindling and a few bigger pieces of wood, stacking it up like a little tepee. I lit the old farmer's match, and the paper quickly caught fire. The kindling started to burn, and then, oops, the smoke was billowing throughout the cabin. I hurriedly started adjusting the little handle on the stove pipe. I know it's called the damper, but that day it was called the hot little sucker on the stove pipe.

Playing with the damper, I finally got a nice fire burning with no smoke. Feeling a new burst of confidence, I was ready to become friends with this hulking black creature of a stove. With my fire burning nicely, I wondered what I should make. After all, I was supposed to be the cook. I knew that the men were working physically hard down in the mining area and needed some good, hardy meals, but I had no idea about quantities. I was used to soup and sandwiches for lunch or maybe a salad. Well, that wouldn't do for two hardworking men. I had a couple of ham sandwiches left over from the day before, and I threw a big pot of noodles together with a can of vegetables, hoping it to be a filling lunch. I don't know if Boese had enough to eat or not, but there wasn't a scrap left over for me, so I thought I might need to plan on more food for their daily lunches.

It seemed that all I had done that day was cook, with little time for my daughter or anything else. Dinnertime fast approached, and I cooked one of the caribou roasts, fried some potatoes, opened a can of creamed corn, and added a fried egg on top of the potatoes. Boese seemed to be pleased because at the end of the meal, he gave a whopping burp, which shocked and rather disgusted me. Later, that evening when I mentioned the incredible sounding burp, Hub explained that to an Eskimo, burping is like saying 'thank you' for a good meal. I never did get used to his loud burping at the end of every meal, and after a short time, it irritated the hell out of me.

That afternoon, while Brandi was napping, I ventured back down into the cellar and took an inventory of Boese's food supply. Our agreement was to split all food costs three ways, so we needed to pay him for the food he had on hand. I found some strange items in that cellar: a whole case of soy sauce, which would probably last a few lifetimes or more, ten huge containers of oatmeal, jars and jars of marmalade, and two cases of ketchup. I hoped we didn't have to split the cost of his inventory because we would never have lived long enough to use some of these goodies. I obviously needed to have a talk with Mr. Boese about paying for his supplies.

A few days after our arrival, I started digging up the ground for my garden spot. I was excited by the richness of the deep dark black soil. I felt certain that, with a little moisture, I should have lettuce by the Fourth of July. My garden wasn't large, but I planted little rows of lettuce, onions, carrots, Swiss chard, and, of course, a few flowers. I also planted a couple of tomato plants I had brought along. With twenty-four hours of sunlight, warm days and cool nights, gardening above the Arctic Circle was no different from gardening in Fairbanks, so I expected a bumper crop of veggies. This little garden area became the lunchtime conversation between us. We discussed how fast it grew, what it needed, and who would be the first to eat the fresh tomatoes.

It was a happy day when we were reunited with the family dogs. Karl, our pilot friend, had been one of their caretakers for a few days in Fairbanks, until he had time to fly them home to us. Looking at the plane when he landed, there sat my dog, Katmai, in the copilot's seat, and Kobuk was huddled up in the back corner of the plane. This was typical of our dogs. Katmai was my spoiled little princess, and Kobuk was the shy working dog of her master.

Katmai had a great love for Brandi and vice versa. As soon as the door of the plane opened, Kat jumped out and rushed to me and began licking Brandi as if she were the best thing in the whole wide world. Kobuk quietly lurked inside the plane, nervously waiting, until Hub gave him a command to 'Come.' These dogs had been our children until Brandi was born ten months previously, and at times, they still felt like our first kids. We were definitely ready for their return.

Hub had already built each of them a nice new doghouse with extra-long chains for a run. They adjusted to their homes quickly, although they howled all night at or with the local wolves and chased the damned porcupines. These became our biggest problem. Our dogs had a love/hate relationship with them and couldn't resist the temptation to chase and catch those spiny devils. During the night, the dogs were always kept on their chains, but in the daytime, if we were outside, they ran free. In the first week, Katmai came back after her freedom run with a mouth filled with hundreds of quills. She had become used to my removing quills from her, but it was still a sad and painful afternoon for both of us. We decided it was better for the dogs and us to let them loose only when we could carefully watch them. However, being exceptionally devious dogs, they still captured several porcupines.

Along with my other chores, I spent the first week making curtains for the windows and drapes to divide the sleeping area from the kitchen. This was quite time-consuming because it was all done by hand. I sure missed my sewing machine, among many other electrical devices. Besides sewing, I kept busy mopping the floor repeatedly, sanding the splinters in the wood, waxing, and re-mopping. It wasn't because I was a fastidious cleaner, but my poor baby's knees were black and had several splinters from crawling around the cabin. The knees of her pants were filthy and were already becoming threadbare. I had brought a small carpet with us, but it was pretty hard to keep a ten-month-old in one area. Not only was she insistent on exploring the entire cabin, but if the door was open, out she crawled. I gave up on worrying about the dirty clothes. My biggest concern was that Brandi loved dirt. As soon as she was out of the door, she was grabbing dirt and shoving in her mouth. She ate more dirt than oatmeal.

After we had been there for a couple of weeks, Hub and Boese flew to Wiseman in Boese's Super Cub to pick up mail and a shipment of food. It was always a quick visit because Boese wasn't a social person and didn't much care for the company of the local men. Wiseman was about twenty miles from our cabin, so it was just a short flight, but one not taken unless it was mail day or something urgent. Mail was delivered twice a month to Wiseman, if we were lucky.

In 1971, the village of Wiseman had a population of four old-timers, one relatively young character, one elderly Eskimo lady, and a family who occasionally spent the summer there. There were about thirty old log cabins, but only these residents' cabins and a few more were being maintained. Charlie Breck, Ross Brockman, Vincent Knor, and Harry Leonard were all old-timers and had been miners or prospectors in that area since the thirties and forties. Ross Harry, the youngster of the bunch, had been a teacher in Fairbanks and had given up the city life to live in Wiseman in 1968. Florence Jonas-Kalhabuk had somehow come to this village traveling with other Eskimos and decided to stay.

The men of Wiseman were a rather strange lot. You would think they would have all gotten together and been close friends, but that was far from the truth. Each person seemed to hold a grudge against one or the other, and there were a lot of little feuds happening weekly.

Old Harry Leonard seemed to be the self-appointed mayor, welcoming committee, and commissioner of the area. It was said he treated his dogs better than he treated people. He even went so far as to set plates for his dogs at the dinner table and had a cemetery next to his house for his former dogs. He arrived in Wiseman in the early thirties, an educated man with a geology degree. With this knowledge, he staked many mining claims throughout the area. When the Alaskan pipeline went through this area, he did exceptionally well selling some of his claims to the pipeline. He and Ross Brockman seemed to have a lifelong feud, neither speaking nor helping each other, no matter what the situation was.

Brockman, a rather quiet man, didn't approve of Harry Leonard's moneymaking ideas, and Harry Leonard seemed to think Brockman wasn't cut out for prospecting and mining. Brockman was a poet and a singer. He didn't own a guitar, so he played along, twanging on a saw and singing his lovely music. He was also a first-class gardener.

When I asked questions about his garden, his eyes lit up, and he became an encyclopedia of Arctic gardening. When I told him about my garden and bread baking, he laughed and said, "You have the makings of a good Eskimo squaw." I took this as a compliment from a man who rarely spoke to anyone and seemed to think quite highly of Mrs. Jonas.

Charlie Breck arrived there in the late forties and was the man in charge of everyone's mail or at least while we were in that area. He seemed to be the most easygoing of all the men and liked everyone. He was able to set aside everyone's differences and didn't fall into their feuds. I heard a cute story about him from one of his friends. It seems that Charlie, in his later years, had gone to Fairbanks to get a hearing aid, which sometimes he wore and sometimes he didn't. One day, while making a huge pot of stew, he couldn't find his hearing aid. A week or more went by, and he was pretty upset by his loss. When he finally finished off the pot of stew—well, there sat his lost hearing aid at the bottom. Then his friend told me, "I wonder how moldy that hearing aid was, 'cause I've seen him scrape the mold off food before."

Ross Harry, the youngster of Wiseman, had been spending a few summers there prospecting for gold and hunting and came to love the wilderness so much, he quit his teaching job in Fairbanks and moved to Wiseman. He, like these older men, grew to love his solitude. Unlike the old characters, he occasionally took a short trip to town, and he also had friends who would fly in to visit, hunt, or prospect with him throughout the summer. Hub was one of those who spent time with him, prospecting for gold, hunting, and wandering the hills. When Ross came to town, he often would stay at our house. He seemed to like my cooking, and I liked to hear his great line of baloney. I guess I could blame Ross for our being at Linda Creek, despite having warned me before we moved, "It's no place for a woman, and it sure as hell isn't anywhere to raise a baby." He was a loyal and wise friend. When Brandi was born, he had Mrs. Jonas make her a wolf parka. He could have easily sold that wolf hide for a good amount of money, but instead gave us a treasured gift.

Florence Jonas may have been the only person in Wiseman whom everyone spoke well of. She was an independent lady and didn't depend on anyone to care for her. However, many of the men would leave an extra quarter of moose or caribou for her if they got lucky with their hunt. She was the last full Eskimo to live in Wiseman until her passing in 1979 at the age of eighty-two. She was so highly respected, a chapel in Wiseman and a nearby mountain were named after her.

The parka Mrs. Jonas made for Brandi was an incredible work of art. Her parka had only the side seams and no other. She certainly knew how to design a child's parka and how to cut a wolf pelt with superior skill. She wasn't just an incredible seamstress, but a lovely hostess as well. On one visit to her house, she gave us a huge bag of caribou jerky. She said it was made especially for Brandi to cut her teeth on. When I left her cabin, Ross Brockman told me, "I wouldn't let your baby eat that because Florence always sprays her meat with Raid to keep the flies off." It was a generous gift, but I gave it to our dog and not Brandi.

During one trip to Wiseman, Hub stopped in to visit with Mrs. Jonas. He asked her what she thought about Brandi eating so much dirt. She asked him, "Baby eat dirt?"

Hub told her, "Yes, she eats dirt. She eats lots and lots of dirt."

She gave a small laugh and told him, "Baby eat dirt, she good baby."

When he returned with this information, he seemed to be relieved. As for me, I didn't feel that great about it. I still ran around cleaning dirt out of her mouth and saying, "No, no, no, baby no eat dirt."

Those mail trips to Wiseman were few and far between for me. Boese seemed to think it was a man's job to get the mail and off he and Hub would fly. Every so often, Hub would take Brandi with him, but there was never room for me. I guess I wasn't too upset about it because I was just happy to be getting mail and other goodies. Every mail day was like Christmas for me, with letters and packages arriving from friends and family. If the mail plane didn't arrive as scheduled, it was a dark and dreary day for me. I lived from one mail day to the next, savoring letters or eating the little treats someone was thoughtful enough to send. Long before the days of email, cell phones, and texting, letters were rather important, but living in the bush made letters extremely significant and cherished. In the evenings, I would keep the lanterns burning to read and reread those wonderful lines someone had sent.

The mail plane also delivered a lot of treasured food, but one thing I never ordered was bread. After being there a week, I had used all the store-bought bread, and it was time to make my first batch of homemade bread. I had made cinnamon rolls many times, but I had never made regular old bread before. Having forgotten to take any bread pans with me, I was relieved to find some already there. I will honestly admit my first batch was more like eating hardtack or crackers than bread. It had to be eaten, though, because there was no other option. As time went by, my weekly bread baking did improve. On one such baking day, two men from the Bureau of Land Management arrived as I was taking those four loaves out of the oven. Being a generous host, Boese offered them coffee and my freshly baked bread. These two men ate two of my four loaves while I sat grimacing, thinking of how soon I would have to do more baking. I enjoyed baking days, except for the fact that the heat from the wood stove raised the temperature in the cabin to that of a sauna. The temperature outside was hovering around the seventies to eighties all June and July, so baking made for a bitching-hot cabin.

The weather had been perfect since our arrival—cool in the mornings and warm in the afternoons. However, sunny weather meant no rain, and no rain was a problem. Our house water barrel was almost empty because much of our water came from rain collected from the roof. Lack of water would have become an issue not only for our house water, but also for the mining operation. Without enough rain, the mining would be much slower. With a little complaining from me, needing water in the house became a top priority. Eventually, the men drove Boese's old truck to the river and brought back house water in fifty-gallon barrels. This job required them to fill five-gallon buckets from the river and then empty them into the fifty-gallon barrels. Back at home, they again filled the five-gallon pails and dumped the water into our hundred-gallon house tank. All I had to do was turn the water faucet inside the house, and yippee, I had water. It's hard to believe we drank water directly from the Koyukuk River without purifying it in some way, but we did. All we did was add a few drops of Clorox to the water tank. No, I didn't even purify Brandi's water either. It seems strange that today we would worry about pollutants, chemicals, and such, creating intestinal problems. We were never sick, nor did we have any problems later.

Our mining operation was in dire need of some good rain. Without water to break up the ground containing gold in the hillside, all the men could do was use the dozer to move the big boulders away from the sluice boxes. This was necessary but didn't produce any gold.

After cleaning the house, cooking, and everything else, I finally had time to spend more time at the 'cut' and see what the men had been doing with their days. Boese explained the operation with a twinkle in his eyes I hadn't seen before and then showed me every step of the process.

Our technique was best known as a hydraulic form of placer mining because of the use of high volumes of water. We had a small dam, which held rain and water collected from runoff of the spring melt. There was a canal, built to carry the water downhill to the cut (mining operation). When there was enough water in the dam, it was run down the canal into a big pipe (which we call the giant), and when the pressure built up in this pipe, it was very, very powerful. The water would cut into the frozen hillside and blast away the rocks and hopefully the gold. The person holding the pipe would then lower the pressure and flush the fresh dirt and gravel into the sluice box. The large boulders and rocks were moved aside by the old D2 Crawler. That awesome old Caterpillar was also used after a good splash and kept the creek in front of the sluice box open so water could flow freely without clogging the end of the box. At that time, the pressure was turned lower, and the opening of the sluice box was given a gentle wash to push the dirt and gold inside the box.

The sluice box was a welded metal box with an opening at about twelve feet wide at the front, but gauged down to about four feet before the riffles began. It was called a 'long Tom' because the length was at least six feet from the opening to the riffles. The riffles were the catch pens for the gold. When it was time for clean-up (collecting the gold), the area beside the entire box was hand-shoveled into the box and carefully washed. At that time, the riffles were pulled, and any gold, sand, and tiny pebbles were deposited in the riffles were then hand-panned. After Boese's show and tell, I became more excited about what they did each day, and our dinner conversations became more interesting.

Brandi, the dogs, and I would take our afternoon walk every day to check out the sluice box to see if there was any gold showing. Then, only a couple of weeks after the backbreaking work, came the fun and exciting part of carrying our buckets of gold, dirt, and sand, from the sluice box riffles up to the cabin to be panned.

I was ready for the gold and had set up three washtubs with water and taken down our gold pans. We were all excited to see what that big hole in the hill had delivered to us. We took time for a cup of coffee, laughing and talking before we started on the serious job of retrieving every grain of precious gold.

Washing the heavy black sand away from the gold was a skill many Alaskans learned early, but I was a little nervous at first because it was the tricky part where the sand was almost as heavy as gold and didn't separate easily. It was encouraging to know that if I lost some gold dust, it could be retrieved in the washtub we were using to pan the gold. After we had panned it out as cleanly as possible, Boese took our pans and put them on top of the cook-stove for a few minutes. He then used an artist's paint brush and, like an artist, swished the remaining sand away from the gold. Being satisfied that the gold was as clean as possible, he took out his gold scales.

I had never seen these scales before because he kept them in his cabin. Boese was happy and proud to show these beauties to us, but then he became quite serious and started polishing each piece. They were a true work of art, just sitting empty on the table, but when he filled the little pans with gold, they became a masterpiece. He spent a long time fiddling with the scales and their weights, and then he would add or subtract the delicate weighs for accurate measurement. When he finished weighing the gold, he asked for our agreement with the measurements. He was a stickler for accuracy and fairness to our contract. We were all in agreement, and we each received the correct share.

After only two weeks of work, we had done an early clean-up because the sluice box wasn't doing an adequate job of catching the gold. It was old and had too many rough edges and cracks, allowing precious gold to slip through. The men agreed it was time to replace it and build a new one. This quick clean-up rendered thirty-five ounces of glittering gold. Most of the nuggets in our mine were rather small: about a half-inch by a half-inch or a little bigger. This was perfect gold to be graded as jewelers' gold, and this size and coloration brought a higher price than the standard thirty-eight dollars an ounce. I'm sure we were all calculating that if this could be done in two weeks, what was possible in two months? I believe it was known as gold fever, and we all caught a little that day.

Boese wasn't only a stickler for his gold measurement; I discovered he wanted everything done his way, and when he wanted it. If dinner was late, I received a lot of noise from him as he cleared his throat, and he would give me the evil eye. The local gossip was that his Eskimo wife got tired of doing all the work and not getting any of the gold. One day, she caught a ride to Fairbanks with another bush pilot and never returned. There were a few days when flying out of there seemed like a good idea to me too.

With the lack of water for the mine and needing new sluice boxes, the men were busy in the shop, welding state-of-the-art sluice boxes and hauling more water for the house. With them working close by in the shop, I thought it was the opportune time for me to experiment with the washing machine I found stored in the cache.

Laundry day was definitely not a simple matter of throwing some clothes in a washer and waiting for the timer to go off so you could put them in the dryer. I was lucky that Boese had an old-time wringer washing machine, and I was happy to have the men around to start the generator. Before I could start the washer, I first had to run what seemed like a mile of heavy-duty electrical cord from the shop to the house. Then I had to heat tons of water to fill the washer and the rinse-tubs, and finally, they would start the generator.

My initial experience with this old beauty was rather fun. After heating a ton of water, I practiced using the handles to operate the washing gear. That worked pretty well with no problems. Next, I experimented with the wringer. I had heard jokes about women getting their titties caught in the wringers. True or not true, I was a little nervous about my hands getting caught, so I used a wooden spoon to push the clothes through the wringer the first few times, but it all worked quite smoothly. I did several small loads of Brandi's clothes and her diapers. Then I drained the machine and added fresh water, so the poo-poo from the diapers was gone. My new fresh water was hot and ready, so in went a load of shirts. I think I only washed them for about ten minutes, or until they looked clean. Next came the wringing of soapy water: rinse, wring, rinse, wring, and finally hang them to dry. It took several hours from beginning to end, but when I finished, I was quite proud of those clean clothes. I did decide it was easier to hand wash Brandi's and my own shirts daily, but the men's clothes and my Levis still needed machine washing about every two weeks.

This old wringer-washer, the generator, the steel for the new sluice box, the truck, and the caterpillar had all been taken to Linda Creek from Bettles. Mr. Boese would go to Fairbanks every winter after freeze-up, place his orders, and arrange for an air-transport to deliver his goods to Bettles. From there, he would use his old Caterpillar D2 Crawler and a sled wagon to haul his heavy supplies back home to Linda Creek. This was a trip of about sixty miles, in the dead of winter, when temperatures often went as low as sixty to seventy below zero. Today, it's possible to drive from Fairbanks to Linda Creek in a few hours using the Dalton Highway, which is locally known as the Haul Road, built in 1974 for the oil fields of Prudhoe Bay. However, back then it wasn't an easy trip. There were no roads, no hotels, nothing except trees, hills, rivers, and simply more vast wilderness. Boese took as long as it took him, with no plans other than safely reaching home with his valuable load of supplies. In 1971, Linda Creek was still way off the beaten track, but Boese had more important mining and living tools than anyone I knew of in the Brooks Range. It made me deeply appreciate the washing machine, the refrigerator, and every special item we had on Linda Creek.

One afternoon, I noted there was an unusual amount of air traffic over our cabin. Later, that night we listened to the Fairbanks news and *Tundra Topics*. A Fairbanks radio station broadcast *Tundra Topics* personal messages to the bush, so we listened for any important message and the local gossip nightly. If you had a message for someone in the bush, all you needed was to call the radio station, and at 8:00 p.m. it was heard throughout the interior of Alaska.

With only a battery-run two-way radio using those big old D batteries, we only listened to it for a short time and for important matters. How I yearned for a little music and would occasionally sneak it on during the day. That night, there was nothing exciting on *Tundra Topics,* but the Fairbanks news reported that the secretary of the Interior was flying over the proposed area for the Trans-Alaska pipeline. That was what our busy air space had been about. This horrid pipeline was scheduled to come right down our front yard. Most of the local people living in the bush and the natives of Alaska were one hundred-percent opposed to this creature, but the wealthy politicians of Alaska were going to develop it, no matter what.

A week later a helicopter landed on our airstrip. These men were surveying for a proposed railroad to the north slope of the Brooks Range to provide passage for the men who would be working on the Alaskan pipeline in Prudhoe Bay. Boese spent about five minutes with them and then demanded that they get off his airstrip. The discussion at lunch that day wasn't something I wanted Brandi to hear. I didn't know Boese ever swore, but he was terribly angry with what was happening to his tranquil and solitude home in the wilderness. I also believed it would the beginning of the end as we knew it on the Koyukuk, and it was a sad day for all of us.

It wasn't all work and no play for me. I took the time out to hunt for wild berries, pan a little gold at times, and go fishing on several afternoons. There were many things I loved about living there, and many I didn't, but it was all a huge learning experience.

One of the things I did learn was how vital being clean was to us. In the city, you turned on a faucet and took a hot shower or bath any time you felt like it. There in the cabin, we had to plan for bath night. Bathing Brandi was a simple job of heating a little water and filling the kitchen sink whenever she wanted or needed a bath. For Hub and me, it wasn't that easy, as we didn't come close to fitting in that little sink. More water was needed to fill the laundry washtubs in which Hub and I bathed. This was a sight to behold; just picture a six-foot man in a little washtub, with his long legs sticking out. Oh, how we laughed as he tried to bathe that long, tall body in that little washtub.

At other times, we would go down to the cut and bathe in the warm water from the giant (the big pipe that delivered water to the mine). After being there for a month or so, Hub built a cute little sauna. He cut small spruce poles from the hillside, dragged them to the location, then cut and notched each log, fitting them together like little toy Lincoln logs. My job was to chink the logs, shoving moss in between the gaps in the logs, like insulation. Everything was done the same way as building a cabin, so it took a little time for it to be perfect. The finishing touch was to cover the roof with a tarp to let out the steam from the sauna and keep out the squirrels and the rain. It even had a small window—for what purpose, other than being cute, I'm not sure. I think Hub was practicing his skills to build a bigger cabin, but I was helping only for the prospect of a delightful, warm, cleaning, sauna. Boese had a small wood stove that we absconded with for the fire.

First, we would get a fire going to heat the rocks on the top of the stove. Once the rocks were hot, we would throw a little water on them, and the steam would roll over our bodies. When it got too hot to bear, we would rush outside and throw a bucket of cold water over ourselves, and return into the steaming sauna. That sauna was like a dream when it got cooler at night, plus we smelled much better after its construction.

Most days were pretty much the same, with the men working in the mining area, repairing the tractor, digging a new outhouse, or some other necessary chore. I found the new outhouse project an interesting, educational, and much-needed endeavor.

It wasn't just a matter of physically digging a deep hole and building a little building to cover it. As soon as the tundra was dug through, the frozen ground was only about eight inches beneath it. That was when the men fired up the Yukon boiler, a wood-burning hulk of a boiler. Then a steam-pipe was attached to the boiler, and steam blew out the tip creating enough heat to melt the ground. It would melt the ice down about six inches at a time. Then they would muck out the melted dirt that had become a slushy mess. This melting and mucking went on until the hole was about eight-feet deep. A wooden cage was then built from local logs, to prevent dirt from collapsing and provide a firm platform for the house to sit on.

Once the frame was in place, an outhouse was placed over the hole. It was christened as the best smelling biffy in the Brooks Range. Inside our little outhouse was a coffee can to hold the toilet paper which keep it dry and prevented the mice and squirrels from shredding it. We also had a can of lye to keep the nasty odors at bay, which wasn't needed as it got colder. If flies or mosquitoes became a significant problem, we hung flypaper, which was an ugly sticky paper that hung from the ceiling.

If only there had been an easy remedy for keeping the mice and squirrels away from all the buildings. Our cache (the storage shed) was a favorite spot for squirrels, and they tore up anything and everything stored there. Finally, war was declared, traps were set, and target practice was an evening event. In the end, the mice and squirrels won.

Early in July, we had tasty fresh lettuce from the garden, and we also had fresh sheep meat. I do know the lettuce was much easier to get than the sheep meat. With only a few packages of moose and caribou left in the freezer, it was time for some fresh sheep meat.

With our spotting scope set up at the cabin, we could view the hillside where sheep often hung out, giving us a decent idea if they were in the area or not. Once we spotted them, Hub would start off immediately. If he was lucky, he would return five or six hours later.

First, Hub needed to cross the Koyukuk River, where a small rickety boat was anchored ashore. Depending on how fast the river was flowing on that day, it could be quite a dangerous crossing in that leaky old boat someone had abandoned years earlier. Once across the river, it was an incredibly steep climb to the top of 'sheep market mountain,' where the prize was expected to be. Within a few hours, we would have fresh sheep meat for our freezer.

No, this wasn't legal then, nor is it today. This was just the standard practice for people living in the bush at that time. Killing for needed meat, not for the sport of hunting, was an acceptable way of life and overlooked by most law enforcement. Linda Creek was almost three hundred miles from Fairbanks, and the Brooks Range wasn't a hot spot for hunting at that time. The only sheep taken in our area were by a few die-hard hunters, the Wiseman locals, and a few Eskimos. Illegal or not, that was what we ate until a moose wandered by or the caribou started their migration.

When Hub returned home with the sheep, he would skin it, and then my job was to cut it into roasts or chops and save the bones for soup. Of course, the bones were later given to the dogs to enjoy, but not a tiny morsel of meat went unused. Once again, I was thankful to have that marvelous freezer to store our meat. Most people living in the bush didn't have this luxury item. Without my lovely freezer, I would have been making tons of jerky, and our meals would have become quite primitive.

In the middle of July, on one of these trips for fresh meat, Hub reported that there was an inch of snow on the mountain where he hunted. The temperatures in the Arctic can be crazier than one ever imagined. It could be in the eighties and still frosty at night. My only concern was my garden, which survived those light frosts until early September, and then sadly, it was hit by too heavy a frost.

With cooler days ahead, it was time to harvest blueberries for fresh blueberry pancakes and dry them for the winter supply. With Brandi in her much-loved backpack we traipsed miles in search of the mother lode of berries.

Boese had recommended a certain area, but we found few there, so I kept going towards the creek. That was when I found not only a ton of ripe berries, but also saw lovely, delicious grayling swimming in every little pool of water.

For the next few afternoons, I returned to the creek with baby on board and fishing pole in hand. It was a nice treat to have fish for dinner. However, the best treat of all was fresh ptarmigan. After spotting several of these delightful little birds, I quickly changed from fishing pole to gun, and we had a savory dinner of ptarmigan that night. Ptarmigan is not only delicious, but also the state bird of Alaska. They're stunning little birds that are brown in summer and turn white in winter. This is the perfect camouflage, making it a challenge for hunters and predators.

One of the cutest things about the willow ptarmigan is its feathered toes. These birds are usually found in small groups in summer but band together by the hundreds in the spring. That day there was a dozen of these delightful little brownish birds scattered throughout the rocks. With the coming of winter, they were also busy eating berries, and moving to the higher country. From our cabin, we could hear their sweet noises which sounded like warbling and then people gargling with rocks in their mouth. I loved their strange sounds, but most of all I loved their flavor.

August 10, 1971 was a historic day. It was Brandi's first birthday. I was shocked by all the packages that arrived on time. It surprised me that so many people understood our mail service and how long it took for mail to be delivered. Later, Hub admitted that he had been hiding her presents from me for weeks. Every time he went to get the mail for the last month, there were special packages addressed to Miss Brandi. It seemed everyone had surprised me and certainly made her birthday special to me.

I may not have remembered her crib, but I did remember to bring a cake mix and party hats. I'm quite sure she was the cutest girl in the entire Brooks Range on that day, all dressed up in a fancy purple frilly dress. It was rather a strange sight to see this little girl dressed to the nines, eating her pink birthday cake, sitting at the table with one old man and her parents with party hats on their heads, being the only guests for such a significant day. Apart from her looking so fancy, one of the cutest and sweetest things was Mr. Boese in his party hat smiling at everything she did. He definitely had a soft spot for this little birthday girl.

After all my concerns about her having presents to open, she set my thinking straight. She didn't much care about what was in the packages or looking at the new toys but quickly passed over everything and chose the empty boxes as her favorite. By crawling, walking, and scooting, she hauled a box outside where she tried to get Katmai into the box with her. The fancy party dress was destroyed, but the little girl and her dog didn't give it a moment's notice, nor did I.

In my journal every day, I recorded the temperature, weather, what I cooked, how the garden was growing, what Brandi did, how the mining was going, how many sheep I could spot, and what the wolf activity was around our cabin.

From the first week after our dogs arrived, they were harassed at night by wolves. From the tracks that were left, it looked like there were three or four prowling close by. They were usually around for only one night, and then they would disappear for a week or so. It was no secret when they were in the area because their howling could wake the dead and start our dogs whining and howling back at them. Later in the summer, I would see one lone wolf circling the hillside along our cabin in the daytime. This old wolf stayed around for a week or more, and then we thought she had gone. Hub hung my gun on a post near the door and told me, "If you see her again, shoot her. Boese has seen her lurking around his cabin as well and has his gun ready. Your gun is loaded and ready to go. If you see her anywhere, take a shot, and maybe she'll leave."

Not only were our dogs still being annoyed by the wolves, but I was being driven crazy with fear of letting them loose for even a minute. I also saw porcupine every day, close to the cabin, and I knew that given the chance, the dogs would find them in a heartbeat.

One horribly sad day, Kobuk escaped and returned with his entire body covered in quills. We spent hours removing as many quills as possible, but there were just too many, and our poor baby was in too much pain. Kobuk was put to rest beside our cabin on Linda Creek in the Brooks Range of Alaska. Katmai was never again left alone to run free. She was kept on a leash from that day forward.

For Brandi's birthday, Hub gave her his old harmonica and a coyote call to play with. She liked the harmonica, but how she loved to blow on that damned coyote call, and its piercing noise drove me nuts. She didn't have much in the way of toys, and she loved it, so I let her blow away.

On a lovely warm afternoon, I had the cabin door open while she happily crawled in and out of the cabin playing on her blasted toy. I happened to look up as she crawled back inside the cabin, and at the doorway directly behind her stood a wolf. I screamed and ran towards the wolf yelling and flapping my arms. Luckily, the wolf turned and started out of the cabin but then suddenly changed his mind. He wasn't going to be scared off by my yelling.

Coming closer, he laid his ears back and snarled at me, acting like a hungry or angry dog. He then crouched down lower on his hind legs and let out a deep rumbling growl. His lips curled up, and he was slyly sneaking closer and closer to my baby. I was sure if I moved too quickly, it would make a lunge for her. I slowly moved between the wolf and Brandi. Oh my god, my baby was so close, and this horrid wolf looked so vicious and deadly. Then I remembered my gun was hanging on the post, right above where I stood. I slowly reached up and brought it down to my shoulder. Never taking my eyes off him, I glared into his eyes, trying to prove I was the alpha male.

Still, he sat crouching with his ears back, ready to pounce, growling and snarling. This gun was loaded at all times, and all I had to do was flip off the safety and pull the trigger. With a mother's rage, I shot that damned wolf right in the doorway of our cabin. Then I grabbed my baby and started screaming. Brandi wasn't the least bit scared until I started yelling. She probably thought it was a nice new dog to play with. Her father arrived a minute after he heard the shot and my screaming. I flatly told him what he could do with the coyote call, the wolf, and he had better be thinking about finding a new cook because my baby and I were leaving.

I was mad at that damned wolf for threatening my baby, but I was more irate at her father, who gave her the god-awful coyote call. He was a hunter and a trapper, and he certainly should have known better. Coyote calls mimic the sound of a dying rabbit, and wolves love rabbits. Even Boese was disgusted by Hub's lack of judgment.

I don't know if the wolf was the honest reason for my threat to leave, or whether it was just the idea of spending the winter in a cabin with my child having no one other than three adults and no children to learn and play with, but we weren't staying there all winter.

Part of my decision to leave was also based on a strange reaction from Brandi towards a couple of men who happened to stop by our cabin. When these two men walked in our cabin, she started screaming hysterically and wouldn't let go of me. As a mother, it registered on me that these were her formative years, and two strangers taught me that I didn't want this reclusive life for her.

After a couple of weeks of heated discussions, I coerced Hub into making plans to go back to Fairbanks and look for a teaching job. We informed Boese of our decision, and naturally, he wasn't happy, but neither was I with the thought of staying for the winter.

Boese flew Hub to Fairbanks a week later, as he had already planned on going there for winter supplies. Hub was lucky with the job hunt and notified me via *Tundra Topics* to get packed, and a plane would pick Brandi and me up sometime in the next week or ten days. Those were several long days with Mr. Boese not speaking to me but still belching after dinner each night.

Not only were they long days, but cold ones too. It had already snowed, and everything was frozen, so I was getting a small taste of what winter would deliver. On the seventh day, happily, I heard the buzz of an airplane. Paul Shannahan from Bettles landed, and I ran out to meet him. When he stepped out of his plane, he told me, "Little lady, get your stuff out here as quick as you can. I'm sorry I can't help you, but I won't enter Boese's cabin, even to help you. Please hurry, because I don't want to be here any longer than necessary." I already had everything ready to go, and Brandi and I were quickly loaded aboard his Cessna 180.

Taxiing down the runway, Shannahan told me the only reason he was there was because Hub had told him it was important that I was picked up and the sooner the better. On the flight to Bettles, he laughed and said, "I don't think it was just important, but more like an emergency to get you out of there. I'm curious how you lasted as long as you did because no one else has ever stayed on Linda Creek for more than a week, except Boese's wife. That man is one ornery old cuss, and we've never gotten along. Last winter, he came to Bettles and told everyone to stay out of his area, or there would be trouble. We had our troubles in the past because he didn't want me hunting wolves in his area, but this time, it was more like a personal threat. I decided right then not to land on his airstrip ever again, but a lady in distress can't be ignored."

Landing in the tiny town of Bettles felt to me like arriving in a cosmopolitan city. There was electricity, running water, and people. Brandi and I spent a couple of days there waiting for a flight to Fairbanks. It seemed her fear of people had sort of disappeared, and she had fun walking around the Bettles Lodge being fed candy by all the Lodge employees. The cook was especially taken with her and wanted to fix her something she would like. I wasn't sure what that was; the only thing I knew she really liked was sheep meat or ptarmigan and mashed potatoes. The cook thought that was pretty funny, but he told me, "Sheep meat seems to be the favorite of all kids from the bush, but I bet she'll really like my moose meat today." He was right. Moose meat became her favorite from that day forward. It was a good thing because I didn't intend to go back to Linda Creek the following summer for sheep meat, gold, or any other reason.

The following chart will show you what our gold was worth when we were mining and at today's price—if we still had it. This is also why the mines in Alaska are back in production after several years of not much mining in the state.

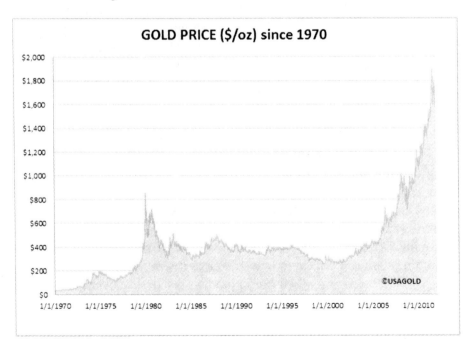

## CHAPTER 13
# RETURNING TO FAIRBANKS

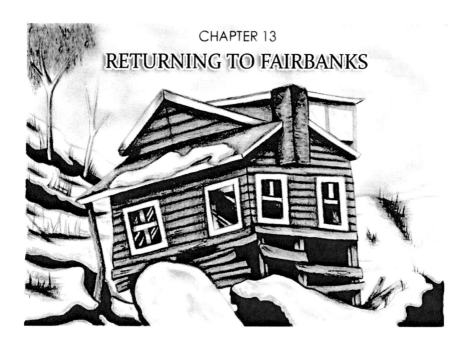

Leaving Linda Creek and returning once again to the civilization of Fairbanks was exciting but not half as easy as I had expected. I forgot we had sold our pickup, put everything in storage, and sixty below zero was fast approaching.

Boarding the flight from Bettles to Fairbanks, the smile on my face must have lit up Alaska, as brightly as the aurora borealis. I was giddy with excitement to be returning to the civilization of Fairbanks, and Brandi and I were the first to board the mail plane. That wasn't difficult because we were the only passengers on that particular day. After a picturesque flight and a few happy giggles, we landed, and Hub was there to meet us. He quickly loaded us into what looked like an antique or a wrecked ten-year-old pickup, and off we went chugging down the road into Fairbanks.

Along the way at every red stoplight, Brandi would point at the light and yell HOT, pushing back in her car seat and grabbing my arm. It finally dawned on me she was afraid it would burn us. In our cabin, everything red was hot, and she had been warned not to touch. I was concerned this was a little too fast an introduction to civilization for her, so we stopped at the Dairy Queen for a quiet moment and ice cream, thinking it would be a delightful treat for all of us. Hub held the cone and pushed it towards Brandi. She pushed her head away, not accepting it. Then he took a little dab on his finger and put it on her lips. She let out a scream, *hot, hot, no, no*. Neither of us dreamed any child wouldn't immediately love ice-cream, but I guess it's a gradual love rather than an in-the-face, new, scary thing. Feeling a little sad for her, we had no problem finishing it ourselves.

Arriving downtown, I ran into a store to do a little quick shopping, while Hub took Brandi to visit her great-aunt. He had only been gone a few minutes when he returned with a screaming child. To see her aunt, they had to take an elevator to her apartment. It was evident Brandi didn't like the people or the elevator. It was a rude awakening to her unaware parents; this little girl had never experienced any of these new and frightening sights. We quickly abandoned what we thought would be a lovely day for all of us and went directly to our new apartment.

As we climbed back into the old beater of a pickup, I asked Hub about what we were doing with this rambling wreck. Before we left for Linda Creek, Hub had cut a deal with the local Chevy dealer where we sold our pickup. Each party agreed on the price offered for the sale, and the purchase price of a new pickup. Somewhere along the line, it became something of a confused mess. With no acceptable vehicles on their lot, we had to wait until they delivered one from Anchorage or the lower forty-eight. How long that would be, no one had a definitive answer. Therefore, we were renting this rig, and it must have come from Rent-A-Wreck because at times it would start and other times not, leaving us stranded until the rental agency would respond. This company was about as dependable as their rented wreck.

The next adjustment was moving into an apartment. Hub had already retrieved our things from storage, and thankfully Brandi had her own crib back. Luckily, the apartment came furnished because we had sold our house in Seward, furniture and all. It was nice to see that he had set the kitchen up with our own items, and we had presentable clothes to wear, other than our old, worn-out mining clothes. Brandi even had a few of her own toys to entertain her, but the only thing that seemed to make her happy was if I held her.

Hub and I had a significant discussion on how to handle the insecurities of her new environment. He was anxious to see friends and get back to living life as we had known it, but that was before Brandi had her own ideas about life. My opinion as a mama was to take it all a little more slowly. I reminded him this little girl has been living in the quietness of the wilderness for the whole of her little life. She had never eaten anything cold and icy, nor had she ever ridden in anything but an airplane. She had never been around anyone other than Mr. Boese, him, and me. I thought all the upheaval was shockingly overwhelming to her. Of course, I won this battle because there was no way Brandi wasn't going to scream her head off when she was scared of anything. I took her for daily walks to the park and let her just watch other children, but still she wouldn't venture out to join them. She soon learned to love ice cream, but only in the security of our apartment.

Returning to civilization wasn't as easy and fun as I had anticipated, even for me. The continued noise was getting on my nerves, and I confess I missed the quietness of the wilderness. Living in an apartment with people walking overhead, everyone slamming doors, loud voices, and living out of boxes was something I hadn't experienced for many years, and so the search for a home began in earnest.

The price of homes in Fairbanks was always rather of a shock due to their exorbitant cost. Looking for a home can either be fun or frustrating, and I was experiencing both. Some of the places I looked at should have been condemned, yet they still wanted more than our newfound gold or bank account would cover.

With luck, I found my ideal home. It sat high on a hill, out of the Fairbanks flood zone, and the builder had done an incredible job of making a unique home. Now, my biggest fear was: if we drove up to the bank in that old beater of a truck we were still driving, why would any smart banker give us a loan? I guess they didn't see the rambling wreck because we came away with signed papers, and we were the owners of a fabulous new home, or so we thought.

Flash Forward one year: one evening, our neighbor, whose property connected to ours, knocked on our door. He had come to inform us his house was sinking and sinking fast. It had been built on an ice lens or giant frost heaves, where water and soil freeze together, and the ice was melting below his house. His living room had been pushed up a foot, in just one short day, and the floor was nothing but an open hole. We followed him home for a look, and it was shocking to see what had happened. He told us that they had heard strange creaking noises for about a week and could hear water running at times, but he had never dreamed anything that disastrous could happen. His elegant living room looked as if a giant bulldozer had ripped it apart and dug a hole in the middle of the hardwood flooring. We could only go into one area of the house because he was concerned the rest of the house was far too dangerous. The last time he looked, one of the bedrooms was protruding out of the side of the house, and their prized swimming pool was cracked, crumbled, and moving into the garage. What can you say to a man who has totally lost his home? We went home and started checking our house for any damage.

Our subdivision held a meeting with the developer because everyone's contracts stated that the entire subdivision had been drilled for ice lenses, which are quite common in Interior Alaska, but none were found. Obviously, they missed some because in one week, our neighbor's house looked as if a glacier has pushed it into a massive pile.

Everyone in the neighborhood started spending any spare moment helping to remove what could be salvaged from his disaster. Trucks were filled with salvage and delivered to his secure new lot in a different area. It was a lovely sight to see neighbors helping neighbors but still a heartbreaking experience for this man and his family. That was when the lawyers came into play, and whopping lawsuits were begun by him and everyone in the subdivision.

I know we felt relieved thinking the ice lens was lower than our property and would not affect us. Then one perfect spring day, I took Brandi for a walk. The snow was still several feet deep, but with longer days and warmer temperatures, it was starting to melt. As we walked up the hillside behind our house, I heard the sound of rushing water. I knew there wasn't a creek close by, so I kept following the noise. The land we had leveled behind our house for cars to park was still packed with snowdrifts, but in the center I could see a rather large hole, and that was where the water noise led me. I don't know what possessed me, but for some reason, I stopped and took Brandi into the house. During her nap, I ventured back outside to see what I could find. I grabbed a long stick and poked in front of me as I walked closer to the hole. I nervously grabbed a rock and pitched it towards the hole. Splash! I got another rock and threw it. Splash! It took way too long to hit bottom.

Being rather stupid, as I was all alone, I lay on my tummy and scooted over to see where this water was. Then I scooted back as quickly as I could crawl and got the hell out of there. This hole was deep and filled with melting ice. I shuddered to think what could have happened if Brandi had ventured into that area or if I had just kept walking. When Hub arrived home that evening, after checking to see what was there, he called a couple of geologists and discussed what we had found. Oh yes, it was another ice lens. They both thought it was far enough away from our house not to affect the structure, but still, we were quite nervous.

We had been in the process of buying another home to remodel and sell, but we sure couldn't afford two homes. With a clear conscience, could we honestly sell this house without disclosing our little problem? Everyone recommended waiting until the snow had melted and seeing what happened with 'the hole.' After the snow had gone, it didn't look quite as alarming. Yes, there was a deep hole behind the house, but it could easily be filled with more dirt and still used to park cars. After checking with lawyers and realtors, we put our house on the market, and it quickly sold. I will admit that every day as I drove past, I would look up on that hill to make sure it was still standing. Even today, it is—thankfully—still there, and the subdivision is filled with new homes, except where the one house went down into the ice field.

## CHAPTER 14
# DELIVERANCE AT TANGLE LAKE

Fishing might not be the only reason I live, but it's certainly *one* of the things in life I live for. To spend a day casting a dry-fly into the water toward a possible fish is as close to heaven as this woman can get.

When Hub offered me a trip to Tangle Lakes and to float the Delta River, I jumped at the chance. But first, I had to find someone I trusted to watch our precious two-year-old daughter, and that put a lot of stress on this mama. I had a hard time leaving her with anyone for only a few hours, let alone four or five days, but the lure of fishing was one reason I considered doing it.

Babysitters I approved of...found. My fabulous and trusted friends, Pat and Lavonne, lovingly volunteered. Our truck, boat, food, lantern, a good book, mosquito spray, fishing and camping gear, and extras were already loaded into the pickup. Hub was the planner and packer of the trip, while I was the worrier about my baby. Everything was ready to go, and then we dropped off our daughter with her babysitters, where I almost changed my mind. However, it had been a while since I had seen my wild, beautiful Alaska, and I was becoming excited to renew the acquaintance. I sure hoped the fish would be biting as well as they were on my last fishing trip.

Leaving Fairbanks on the Richardson Highway, the first thing you would come to was the cute little town of North Pole where the Santa Claus house sat alongside the road. It was rather a strange little town, wholly focused year-round on Christmas and Santa, and it always made me smile. Farther down the Richardson, there are many perfect spots to fish and fairly good ptarmigan hunting too. Being in a hurry to start our float, we didn't take the time to fish along the way, but we did stop at several little roadhouses.

I had traveled down the Richardson Highway hundreds of times before becoming a mama, but this time everything looked fresh and new to my eyes. However, when we passed the famous Black Rapids on the Delta River, I again said, "God, I hope I never end up in that water!" They were the most frightening rapids I had ever seen. I was thankful our float down the Delta would end before this horrid black, icy cold, roaring water. Today, it's classed as a level IV-V, and it's still as brown as mud and scary as hell to me.

I knew two young men who almost lost their lives on that ugly river, and listening to their tale of survival was chilling. These men had been camping and floating the area for a couple of years and knew this water quite well. However, bad things can happen even to an experienced river rider. After a successful hunt across the river, they needed to cross back to their truck. Thinking they had plenty of distance before Black Rapids, they found out they were mistaken. Before they knew it, they were being swept downriver and thrown every which way in one huge swell after another. The sheep they had killed earlier was tossed out of the boat. Next, their oars were lifted out of their oarlocks, and all they could do was hang on to the ropes they had tied inside the boat. With a crazy stroke of luck, they were finally pushed to the edge of the river where they hit a huge rock. The boat was destroyed, but they both scrambled to shore and somehow survived. I knew just by looking at this nasty stretch of water, I never wanted a closer look.

After reminiscing about our friends' harrowing experience, we felt a beer break was in order. Besides wanting a beer, Paxson Lodge was my favorite roadhouse. It was a little fancier and much bigger than most but still purely Alaskan, with huge moose horns hanging on every wall and friendly people to chat with. Typically, roadhouses were originally someone's home alongside the highway. In the old days, they might have served as restaurants, bars, grocery stores, or even brothels. They were a necessity for the gold-rush men and women. In the late sixties to early seventies, they were an Alaskan treasure, serving travelers as well as the local community. Each one was unique, and I wanted to stop at every one of them. Some roadhouses were noted for their blueberry pie, some for the best moose stew in the area, and others for their sexy go-go girls.

After our beer break at Paxson, we took the Denali Highway (the term highway was a whopping exaggeration) for about twenty miles of graveled, pot-holed road to Tangle Lakes. Once there, we set up a small camp and loaded our boat for a three- or four-day float. Our plan was to do a little fishing in Round Tangle and then set off early the next morning to have time enough to make the portage.

Tangle Lakes consist of the Long, Lower, Round, and the Upper Tangle. They're a sixteen-mile chain of lakes, connecting by streams and all leading to the headwaters of the Delta River. Good fishing could be had in all the lakes, but Round Tangle was where we began our float to the Delta River.

Fishing in the lake without a motor was a rather useless exercise. With just paddles to move us around, we were limited to fishing where the fish were smarter and others had already fished. It didn't matter to me, as I was eager to loosen my arm and renew my casting skills. It was wonderful to light a small fire and burn up a steak rather than sit in a fancy kitchen where I could cook my steak to perfection. The open air with a campfire sending smoke in my eyes and mosquitoes swarming over us could beat a Hawaiian vacation anytime. However, I won't lie; sleeping on the ground in our tiny two-man tent wasn't better than my comfy bed at home.

We started off in the early morning, paddling for what seemed like an hour across the lake and finally hit a current of the river to push us along. This part was fast-running, with big boulders and shallow areas where our boat was scraping the bottom. It didn't take long to run the mile or so, and you could feel the quick drop of the river. We knew we had to watch for the sign marking the portage, or we would die going over a big waterfall. Back then, the signage was a handmade, small wooden board nailed on a post, saying 'WARNING—PORTAGE HERE.' Seeing it, we both paddled like crazy to get to the shore. We dodged the big boulders, fought the current, and pulled into shore, safe and sound

My arms were totally exhausted from paddling, but for some reason there was no time to rest. We began the climb, drag, huff-and-puff job of hauling our not-so-light fiberglass boat up and down a half-mile of the so-called trail. It was a nasty climb over steep, rocky, slippery wet ground.

At times, we lost more ground than we gained, with the boat sliding back down the trail until a boulder stopped its descent. We tried every way imaginable to haul that boat up this steep trail. We pushed, then rested, pulled, rested, cussed, dragged, more cussing. Finally, we reached the summit, where it really got interesting once we started down. The boat went slip-sliding rapidly downward, crashing over the top of me. Much more cussing could be heard. After the rapid descent of both boat and woman, we then made a couple of trips back and forth retrieving our supplies.

With both of us totally exhausted, we camped at the edge of the river and did a little fishing. It was a perfect spot to loosen up my casting arm and listen to the quietness of nature. The faint roar of the falls crashing in the distance became our background music.

The shallow rocky rapids for the first mile or so were listed as only a class II float but were still not for the faint of heart because of all of the boating debris scattered on the shore. Seeing many parts and pieces of wreckage along the shore made me reconsider my decision to go on that adventure. "This isn't what a mother should be doing," said a little voice inside my head. I kept wondering whether the owners of all that abandoned equipment ever got out of there. Had they capsized at the falls or along that very spot?

Just as I imagined the worst, the water became slow and tranquil, the most perfect water I had ever seen for grayling habitat, and my worries disappeared. That was what I had gone on the trip for. With my fly rod ready, I stopped to see what type of hatch was out. I decided a mosquito was always a sure bet and quickly tied one on. Being a rather competitive woman, I wanted to be the first to catch the big grayling I could see feeding on the far shore. It didn't seem to matter whether I used a mosquito or some crazy new fly; it was hit after hit, almost like fishing in a hatchery. I was in fishing heaven.

I did hook that big old fish on the far shore. The barbs were already cut off all my hooks, which made for a quick and gentle release. That ravishing beauty with its huge dorsal fin looked like a small sailfish from Mexico, minus its beak.

It's said that the dorsal fin of a grayling can cure a toothache if you just chew on it. This fish is not only beautiful but medicinal. The skin along his gill plates was silvery colored, with black and almost red spots, but his main body was iridescent with blues, pinks, purples, all blending in the glimmering sunlight. His blackish-purple colored dorsal fin was magnificent and completely out of proportion with his body. The dorsal was so large, it swept over almost his entire body. I'm sure that's what makes him fast enough to grab a free meal, and I was lucky that this time his meal was my funny-looking shredded mosquito. He looked about eighteen inches long, or that was my honest measurement, not a fisherman's measurement. The Alaska Fish and Game report that graylings are the slowest-growing game fish in Alaska. A twelve-inch fish may be five or six years old, whereas a nineteen-inch may be at least ten years old. I believe I had caught quite an old man, and he would live to tell his grandchildren about his escape. I hoped his survival and long life was true.

People who have read about Alaska say, 'It sounds like there's a moose behind every tree, caribou wandering the city streets, and a fish on every cast.' Well, that day it felt like 'the fish on every cast' was true, and it was perfect. We had twelve miles and two days of this to-die-for fishing. We slowly floated down this enchanting river, seeing eagles and dozens of ravens overhead, river banks full of various flowers, cooking over a campfire, laughing, bragging about the biggest, or the most fish, and just loving the beauty of Alaska.

On the morning of the third day, we put the fishing gear away and wrapped a tarp around our supplies, and then I put on my life jacket. This would be the end of our crystal-clear water and good fishing. Our map showed that Eureka Creek, which is a glacier-fed creek, entered about a quarter mile past where we were camping. It was sad to see these two rivers merging, one clear, and the other dark and silt-filled from the glaciers. With the dirty water also came sandbars and many small channels, creating slower-moving water. It was to be about seven more miles before we hit Phelan Creek, where we planned to pull out. We expected to be home by our daughter's bedtime.

This part of the trip wasn't that much fun—not a nice tranquil float like the day before. We had to keep watching for the best channel because some were so shallow, the bottom of the boat would drag.

I was positioned in the front of the boat to be the spotter for the best channel, shallow areas, and sweeper of trees or rocks. Suddenly, the river quickly dropped, and ahead was a huge whirlpool. In a flash, our boat was like a champagne cork popped into the air. When we hit the edge of the whirlpool, the boat was airborne at least ten feet in the air, with me hanging onto the side.

Hub had told me in the past that if the boat ever tipped over, I should hold onto the side and not let go, no matter what. As the boat flew out of the water, I grabbed the side as I had been told. When the boat came back down from its flight, it was on top of my head with the tarp holding me down and my life jacket pushing me up. The water was so dark, I couldn't see which way was up or down. I felt along the boat, but instead of going across it, I guess I was going down the length of it.

I knew what was happening, and it just seemed to be a simple job of either getting the tarp off or diving below it. There was no way I was going to dump my life jacket, but I knew it was the main problem at that moment. It wouldn't allow me to dive below the tarp and yet was also keeping me from being swept away. I was quite surprised I wasn't freezing or gasping and choking on water. I wasn't scared to death. I was just really pissed off that I couldn't see the sky. I didn't mind the black water or the cold, and I remember thinking, "This is a horrid way to die, not seeing the sky." It was interesting to me that our little boat had become so long, and I was totally amazed at how long I could hold my breath. Then my thoughts turned to my daughter, and I focused on her pretty little face, with a huge smile showing four new teeth. Suddenly, I felt a

big hand grab my life jacket and start yanking me through the water.
I was a little terrified by this sudden rush of power and afraid to see
who or what was pulling me through the water. My first thought was
"This must be God yanking me up, and I must be dead."

Then Hub threw me on the top of the upside-down boat and told
me to hang on. There was nothing to hang on to, only the wet,
smooth, and slippery fiberglass. I was shaking so hard from the icy
water, and my fingers weren't working. "If I go back in, I'll never
make it." I managed to say, "But don't worry, that's okay. It's not
too bad in there."

He started yelling at me, "Hold on, don't let go. You can do it,
just don't let go. Goddammit, Donna, I couldn't find you. I told you,
always stay with the boat. When I swam back to the boat, you
weren't there. The only thing I could see was something orange. God
damn you, hold on! You can't let go!" Hub kept yelling as he tried to
pull us to shallow water.

As we got our footing and walked towards a sandbar, our boat hit
a huge rock in the fast current and was swept away. It was resting
against a rock in the deeper water. Oops, the only thing we had was a
boat floating down river with no paddles; a man with one boot; a
woman who was so cold, she kept going back into the glacial water
to feel warmer, and almost no hope of any help.

When we got ashore, Hub explained what took him so long to get
back to me. When the boat had flipped over, he had started to swim
for shore, but his boots had filled with water and were slowing him
down. Finally, he kicked one off. Then he looked around and
couldn't see me alongside the boat, so he swam back to the boat, but
all he could see was something orange. He grabbed it and pulled it
up. Luckily, it was my orange life jacket and me.

Our boat had stopped, and we saw it was still hanging on the rock
not too far from where we were safely standing on land. We knew
we needed our boat to get out of this mess. The reality of walking
out was nearly impossible. I quickly volunteered to go back into the
icy water to retrieve our beloved boat because it was warmer than
the cold wind on land, and I had the only life jacket. Hub was pacing
back and forth yelling at me, "You can't stay in the water. Damn it,
pay attention to what I'm telling you, Donna. You can't stay in the

water too long, or you'll die." He then grabbed my shoulders and gave me a good shake and firmly told me, "You'll get hypothermia and go into shock. Do it quickly and get out. If you can't do it, we're totally screwed because right now, it's just you, me, and getting that boat."

Wanting the warmth of the water, I was off in a flash. Looking back, I would say I was already in shock because all I wanted was the warmth of that dirty, black, icy water. Walking out across the shallow area wasn't that difficult, but I didn't find the warmth I was searching for. Soon, I was in deeper water, floating towards the boat and feeling a little warmth spread through me.

When I got there, I burst out laughing, which I'm sure made Hub think I had completely lost track of reality. What made me laugh was that the book we had brought along—Deliverance—was floating alongside the boat. It all seemed too bizarre: being there on that river, in the wilderness, and reading a book about men floating a river, fighting for survival. At that moment, Deliverance seemed like the reality of what we were up against, minus the mountain men or, hopefully, minus those wild, crazy men.

I pulled myself together and quit laughing, grabbed the boat, and pushed off upstream as hard as I could push. I was able to pull the boat back across the channel, and at last—boat, man, and woman were once again on dry land.

Then Hub dropped the big bomb on my non-functioning head. "We can't stay here. There's no wood or anything on this sandbar. We have to leave the boat and swim across to the other side. That's our only chance of surviving. We have to have the shelter of those trees, or the wind will kill us."

I snickered and declared, "I am not (f-ing) swimming across to the other side." Many cuss words were exchanged. "You know I can't swim for shit, and I'm not taking this life jacket off. I know what will happen if I try to cross that swift water, I'll just float away, and you won't be able to do anything about it but keep swimming. You know you can't swim and pull me along. Go to hell, because I'm going back in the water to warm up."

As we had this ridiculous conversation, we both spotted a miracle at the same time. We started screaming our lungs out, jumping up and down and waving like crazy people.

We had been on the Delta River for three days and four nights and hadn't seen another living, breathing soul. Then like magic, down the river came a wonderful aluminum boat with four people in it. But...they kept going. They didn't even seem to notice us. How could they pass us by? We kept screaming and running to get closer, but they floated past us like they had never seen us. By now, our screams had turned to some pretty nasty cuss words, and tears were streaming down my face. When their boat was at the far end of our sandbar, they pulled in. One of the men slowly got out of the boat and nervously walked towards us. When he got up to us, with a shaky voice and tears in his eyes, he kept saying over and over, "Oh my god, oh my god, we thought we were going to die here. You've saved us. Thank God we could stop."

I thought this must be the most crazed person I had ever come across. Maybe he truly was the crazy mountain man from Deliverance. What could he be thinking? How had our rescuer become the rescued? He thought we had saved him from disaster. There we were with a boat, no paddles, and two frozen wet people in the middle of nowhere. Save them? Yes, oh yes, we will after we get in your boat, and maybe borrow some dry clothes, drink a little warm coffee, and possibly wrap a dry blanket around us.

Our rescuers were two doctors and their wives who had never floated a river in their lives. They had been told the Delta was a nice little Alaskan river for an easy float trip. They were new to Alaska and stationed at Eielson Air Force base near Fairbanks. These people were so scared of the river, they hand-lined their boat the entire twelve miles. This meant one man would walk on shore with a rope tied to the front of the boat. The other man had the back of the boat tied to him while the boat drifted downriver close to the shore. These two men were so scraped and bruised from walking through the undergrowth alongside the river, they looked like they had done battle with a grizzly bear. When they saw us, they didn't know how to paddle ashore to help us. Neither of the men knew how to maneuver the boat because they had only been inside it for the last mile, rather than walking it downriver onshore.

The wives had spent four days sitting in the boat, crying and thinking they all would die. They had been worried the entire trip that if they did happen to make it to the take-out point, how would they ever survive in faster water? They all knew that if they missed the take-out, it immediately became a fast and deadly river. They were celebrating that they had been saved. I let them think what they liked. I was only thinking of seeing my baby again and hoping I didn't crack all of my teeth from the severe chattering I couldn't stop.

I hardly remember what these people looked like. I didn't care who they were. I could have been riding with the crazy men from Deliverance, and I would have been happy. I quietly sat in the boat drinking a warm cup of coffee and staring out at the water. One of the doctors told the women to keep rubbing my face and hands to warm me, which irritated the hell out of me, but it was the best they could do other than give me the clothes they were wearing. Sadly, they had tipped their boat over several times and had nothing dry either.

With Hub oaring like a pro, we soon made the take-out point with no problem. These wonderful people, whom we had saved, had a van waiting for them. At last, I had a blanket to warm me up, plus the car heater on full blast. When the men had loaded their boat, one doctor came to check on me again. Looking extremely concerned and speaking very precisely and slowly, he said, "I'm very worried about you. You haven't said one word this whole time. Can-you-talk? Can-I-get-you-something?"

"Yes," I replied "I'd like a shot of whiskey—and I don't even like whiskey."

We all traveled back to Tangle Lake, where our truck was parked. When we got there, the doctor wanted to know if he could do anything to repay us for saving their lives. That was when I started to laugh hysterically, and he was really concerned about me. I think at that point Hub pushed me into the truck and explained to the doctor, "She's just happy we could help you." Even today, thinking about that can make me laugh hysterically. "We saved them?" It may be the best joke of all time.

After they departed, we drove back down the Richardson Highway to retrieve our boat, which we had towed downriver behind the craft of our 'rescuers.' Everything was back in order, and we were all alive.

Hub asked, "So do you still want a shot of whiskey?" He knew I hated the smell of whiskey, let alone drink it.

"Yes I do! The only way I know to get this horrid taste out of my mouth is with something nastier. My father always claimed it would warm the heart of an iceberg. I think it'll be a big shot of Early Times, his favorite drink. No, maybe I'll have them heat it up first."

We returned to the Paxson Lodge for my shot of whiskey. While Hub ordered my hot whiskey, I went to the washroom to clean up a little. When I looked in the mirror, I became as concerned as the doctor had been. How had all these people looked at me with a straight face? My hair was pink. I mean really, really pink. It also had clumps of dirt and globs of gooey stuff wrapped in it. After a few minutes of embarrassment and laughter, I grabbed a bar of soap and scrubbed, and scrubbed. It was still pink. My bleached blonde hair had somehow absorbed the minerals from the water or something. Maybe I went into shock. You hear of people's hair turning grey overnight from a sudden shock. I guess mine turned pink. Suddenly, that shot of whiskey sounded better and better.

Not being a practiced or good drinker, it wasn't long before I was feeling the effect of the nasty whiskey. Perhaps the shock of the cold water or the reality of coming close to dying was playing a part, but all I wanted in this world was to go home and hold my daughter. Being halfway smart, we decided driving home late that night was simply out of the question. We drove a short distance out of town and up to a hillside, where we parked to spend the night. We figured we would both sleep in the cab of the truck. Sometime during the night, this didn't work for me, and I climbed out of the truck and into the soft tundra. I'm sure I rested peacefully there for several hours.

When I awoke, I was shocked at how filthy dirty I was. My entire body was dense black. I laughingly thought this might go nicely with my pink hair. I was a little embarrassed because I thought I had cleaned up a little better the night before, but I was still a nasty dirty sight. As I moved, the black dirt left my body and became a buzzing mass of mosquitoes. Instead of black, I was a swollen mess of red welts. I wondered if I had any blood left after the mosquitoes had drunk their fill throughout the night.

When we returned home, the pink hair and the huge red welts covering my body didn't bother my daughter one tiny bit. As for me, I was in heaven just to see her and hold her in my arms again. I quickly forgot the mosquito-bites, pink-hair problem and felt very lucky to be sitting in my home holding her in my swollen arms, looking at the man with the big gnarly hands, who had pulled me from that icy water.

Maybe becoming a mother had turned me into a not-so-brave, outback-wilderness woman, but this mama was staying home for a good long time, even if the fishing was reported to be excellent.

CHAPTER 15
# THE GREAT WHITE BEAR

In 1972, six hundred people were able to obtain permits to hunt polar bear in Alaska. This drawing included state residents and non-residents of Alaska. I had applied for a permit every year from 1968 until 1971, and I became one of those six hundred fortunate people. I know some non-hunters may find this disturbing, but back then they weren't on the endangered species list, and I was a hunter. The polar bear was said to be the most dangerous hunt on the North American continent. Like any born hunter, I was excited to have one of the exclusive permits.

Polar bears are described as the largest of all land carnivores and the most dangerous to hunt. I believe this to be true because they have no known enemies, and they fear nothing. They're larger and more confrontational than the barren ground grizzly and as large as most Kodiak brown bears.

Thinking back to killing that horrible, nasty grizzly in the Brooks Range and to the fear and adrenaline raging through my body as I faced him, it seemed strange even to me, but I was still excited to hunt this big white shadow of a bear.

After the excitement of opening my hunting permit, I calmed down and started serious preparation for that once-in-a-lifetime hunt. First, I contacted a few well-known bush pilots who guided polar-bear hunters, and from these well-recommended pilots, I chose Pete Merry.

Pete had been a pilot since 1949 and had flown more hours over the north and south side of the Brooks Range than anyone I had ever heard of. He had also guided hunters out of Barrow for many years, which was what I wanted. Pete, being a super-nice man, didn't hesitate to accept me as one of his hunters. Unlike some of the guides, who made me feel as if it were a male-only club, Pete welcomed me. He had already taken his wife on a polar-bear hunt several years earlier, and he thought it was just fine for a woman to want to hunt bear. We agreed on a date when he was available, a price, and he gave me this advice, "Just make sure your gun will fire at thirty or forty below because it will be cold." We discussed what I had hunted before and the caliber of my gun. He said, "It sounds like you're a crack shot, and your .350 Remington Magnum will certainly do the job. Now we just have to find you a nice, big, white bear."

I did prepare my gun as Pete had recommended and checked it would fire properly at forty below on several occasions. Hub would drive me to a shooting area on the side of the Fox highway, and I would step out into the minus forty or fifty degree weather. I would fire three shots, then reload and shoot again. I froze, but my gun fired just fine. Not only was I checking to see if my gun fired properly, but I had to make sure my shooting skills were on target, even while shaking in the freezing Arctic cold.

On one such day, while practicing in those piercing cold temperatures, I returned from my shoot-out with the targets to feel a burning-hot, frostbitten ear and my fingers looking like icicles. I had hunted in minus forty below for caribou without freezing anything, but on that day, there was a wind, and my stocking cap and shooting gloves weren't adequate. Today, that poor old ear is still brown on the edge, like a burned piece of toast.

After shopping for a little better protection from the Arctic winds, I next had to make arrangements for a room at the Top of the World hotel in Point Barrow. Once reservations were secured, I reserved my spot on Wien Air, packed my Arctic gear, and arranged a babysitter for my two-year-old daughter. Leaving her was the most difficult job of all.

Off the three of us went to the airport for a quick goodbye and a small cry, not from my daughter but from me. As I wiped a few tears away and saw who the pilot of that day's flight was, I couldn't help but smile. Karl Maerzluft, a friend who had also flown us into Linda Creek, was my pilot. I had the honor of sitting up front, and as we flew north, Karl pointed out the familiar and unfamiliar area below. It was a treat to have someone I knew show me to my hotel and introduce me to the owner.

Point Barrow in Alaska, and the Top of the World hotel are definitely not like taking a Hawaiian vacation. Barrow is located three hundred twenty miles north of the Arctic Circle. It records three hundred twenty-four days a year with freezing temperatures. The recorded population in 1970 was about two thousand. I'm not sure where all those people lived because it seemed much smaller than that.

As I walked from the hotel to the grocery store never seeing another person on the street, I wondered where everyone was. However, the grocery store was packed with people, most buying a six-pack of Coca-Cola or cigarettes. They may have all been there to get warm, but I think it was also just a spot to gather and visit with the neighbors. It was a tiny little shop but carried all the necessities and not much else. I bought bread, ham, cheese, and a tiny jar of mayonnaise, and if I remember, it took all of my twenty dollars. This was what I ate the entire time I was in Barrow, or in the air scouting for bear. There was a restaurant in town, but it was never open when I was on the ground. We did always have hot coffee, thanks to Pete. I never did find out where he got our thermos filled, but it was always full—a cherished little treat.

The Top of the World hotel was certainly nothing fancy, but I remember being quite surprised by how nice it was. This was Point Barrow, Alaska, and in 1970, not much of Alaska was fancy. There were five or six rooms and a little front-desk area, and that was about it. My room had twin beds with extra blankets and was nice and toasty warm. That bed and being warm were all I cared about after sitting in a very chilly plane all day. I rated my room a five-star for a comfortable bed and those wonderful warm extra blankets.

Our hunting day usually started around 9:00 a.m., when Pete and Cleo would crank up the Super Cubs and I would climb in for a day of flying over nothing but white snow and ice. Pete and I were in one plane and his partner, Cleo McMann, in another. Each man flew Super Cubs on skis and flew side by side most of the time or within sight of each other. We flew all day looking for bear or bear tracks until my eyeballs ached, my neck was stiff, and my butt frozen.

On our first day out, we did see a couple of mamas with babies but no lone, big, single males or older barren females. On the first night, the men returned a little disappointed, but other than being cold to the bone, I thought it was a wonderful experience just to see those incredible white mamas with their babies.

The next morning I asked Pete, "How far did we fly yesterday?" He just smiled and said, "I guess not far enough. Today will be better. We're going out a bit farther, and I feel lucky." With that answer, I climbed into the icy frozen seat, buckled my seat belt, and off we went, eyes glued to the white terrain. Flying over nothing but solid ice may sound rather boring, but the sights below were breathtaking. The ice colors alone were surprising, ranging from snowy white to blues of many colors, and the upheaval of the ice floes were incredible. It was difficult to judge how high the pressure ridges were from the air, but many appeared like mini-skyscrapers of white and blue.

With the noise from the engine, it was hard to hear Pete as he explained the importance of the ice and the pressure ridges. I think he said, "Normally when we spot a bear we want to take, I'll land behind one of those big walls of ice, and Cleo will stay in the air to make sure we land okay and that the ice is safe. Then Cleo will land behind another ridge, and we'll all sit and hope Mr. Bear keeps coming our way. If he doesn't keep coming towards us, we'll stalk it as far as you can walk, or we'll get back in the plane and do it all again until that bear is yours." It all made sense to me after spotting the bears the day before and seeing how we could easily hide behind those massive ridges.

While I was straining to listen, my eyes were glued to tracks below us. Tapping Pete on the shoulder and yelling, "Tracks," little did I know he had been following them for several minutes and yelled back to me, "Those are looking fresh, and they're a good size. This might be the one for you." Off in the distance, I could see the sun hitting a small, shimmering golden bear, but as we got closer, the whiter and bigger it became. That's when Pete yelled, "What do you think? It isn't a huge one, but boy, it sure is a pretty one. You won't find a nicer hide than that bear, but it's your call."

This would be our last attempt of the day, as it was getting late, and we would have to return to Barrow soon. I screamed at Pete, "Let's take it." And with those words, my heart started racing, and my hands were shaking. If you're a hunter, you know what that feeling is. Thankfully, I would have some time to calm down and get ready for the hunt, while Pete looked for the right spot to land. From where I sat, I couldn't see the bear any longer, but I knew I was in the most capable hands of any bush pilot and polar-bear guide around. So I sat back and just hoped my shots would hit their target.

The plane landed safely, and Pete motioned to be quiet as we climbed out. As he pointed in the direction to go, we slowly climbed to the top of the giant wall of ice. At the top, we lay on our bellies and silently waited for the bear to arrive. Oh my god, he was right there in front of me, walking broadside at maybe only a hundred and fifty yards when he came over the ice ridge. This massive white bear was breathtaking as he leisurely strolled across his home of frozen terrain, with no concern for any known predators.

I took my gun off safety, braced my arm, and tried to pretend it was only target practice. With my hand shaking a little, I took careful aim. I had his front shoulder in my sight and then aimed just a little in front of that shoulder, hoping for the best shot. Gently squeezing the trigger, *boom,* roared my gun, and I quickly ejected the empty shell to reload. I had hit him in the right spot, and he was down.

Pete started laughing with delight and said, "That should do it, but we'll give him a few minutes to make sure he stays down before we go get him." Then he yelled to Cleo, "No need to load your gun. She took care of him." Pete had taken enough bear hunters out to know that when the adrenaline stops, the hunter needs a little time to calm down, and so we sat for a few minutes, talking about my bear, my gun and how powerful it was, and even had a cup of coffee. I really wanted to jump up and see this bear up close, but I knew enough to always listen to the pro, and so we sat.

Both Cleo and Pete congratulated me on a perfect shot, and both agreed it was one of the best hides they had seen. These two professional guides quickly prepared the bear for transport back to Barrow, while I watched and jabbered away with excitement. I kept telling them, "I can't believe you knew exactly where the bear would come and where I should lie down. You two are the best guides in the world, and you should be famous. Wow, that's a beautiful bear. Oh my god, you guys, this is just amazing." Every now and then they would look at me and laugh. Being hunters themselves, they understood my excitement and appreciated it.

Arriving back in Barrow, we delivered my bear to a little house filled with several Eskimo women. Pete had made arrangements for the local ladies to scrape the fat and clean the hide for shipping to Jonas Brothers in Denver, where a bear rug was to be created. This group of women only charged twenty-five dollars for this nasty job of fleshing, scraping, cleaning, and getting covered in bear grease. However, all I saw from these delightful ladies were smiles the entire time, while they chatted and worked. One of the ladies told me they were happy to be preparing a bear that beautiful for a woman hunter, and only one hole in the hide was very good, not full of holes like some people took in to them.

I don't know if it was because of our successful hunt or just a coincidence, but there was a big potlatch (celebration) that night with food, singing and dancing, and the legendary blanket toss. This was my first experience at a real potlatch, not one performed for tourists. The dancing and drumming was filled with joy and excitement, but the blanket toss was the most fun. Everyone in the hall joined together to toss young men into the air as high as we could bounce them on the walrus hide. It was almost like a kid on a trampoline, only we were throwing a boy into the air instead of him jumping. It had been an incredible day, and the night of celebration was a wonderful climax to an excellent hunt.

After a successful and interesting adventure, I was anxious to return to Fairbanks and see my baby. Hub and Brandi picked me up at the airport, where we waited for my big burlap bag of bear to unload. We stood around waiting and waiting. Getting a little nervous, Hub went to find out from the ticket office where my bear was. Their response was, "Everything from Barrow has been unloaded."

Hub grabbed my arm and told me, "Hurry, we need to get going." I wasn't leaving without my bear, but he was still insistent on leaving. As we jumped into the truck, he said, "I know what's happened to your bear and where it is. This happened to someone I know, and Karl has also mentioned how many trophies surprisingly go missing. I'm sure it's somewhere stashed in one of the hangars." He was right; at the first hangar, back in a corner with a few burlap sacks throw over it, was my hidden bear hide that someone wanted for themselves or to sell. There wasn't a soul around to answer questions, but neither of us cared as long as we had found it. We loaded my bear, which still had my name tag on it, into the truck and went home to celebrate my hunt and for me to get some love from my daughter.

This incredibly beautiful bear was made into a rug. The bear meat was given to the natives of Barrow, and a few extra dollars were spread around the community. I'm quite sure I was the last white woman to hunt and kill a polar bear in Alaska because hunting by airplane was discontinued that year, and the law remains today. I don't know if that makes me famous or not, but I do know I was one lucky woman to have had this amazing experience.

Perhaps you're thinking back to the statement about the most dangerous hunt in North America and wondering what's the big deal about this hunt? Maybe you're thinking, "If a woman can do it, I could too." Please remember I had the best guides in Alaska with years of experience. I've hunted all my life and had already shot a nasty, ugly, old Grizzly bear, plus I had a big bear gun and two more to back me up in case of an emergency.

I still believe it's the most dangerous hunt, and you may too if you ever flew out fifty miles over frozen or semi-frozen ice in a Super Cub. Then, hopefully, you land on solid ice, rather than ice that's breaking up. Next, you go on foot to find the largest breed of bear in North America that isn't afraid of anything because he has no predator other than man and knowing that if he sees you, he'll come to devour you because anything that moves is food. You may also freeze to death quickly if things go wrong with the plane, the ice, or the bear. It's all a crap shoot when hunting for the great white bear, and I was one of the lucky ones to succeed.

Cleo McMann was later written up in the National Geographic magazine as being the oldest flying bush pilot. I believe he was still flying at seventy years of age.

Pete Merry lives in Fairbanks. He was still working and flying when I last heard from him. Thank you, Pete, for helping with the details of our successful hunt together. I still believe you're two of the most incredible guides in Alaska.

CHAPTER 16
# PRUDHOE BAY OIL

The Alaskan gold rush of the 1800s was a colorful part of history books, but nothing compared to what would take place in the next century. In 1968, Alaska experienced another gold rush, only this time it was for black gold, Texas tea, Oklahoma cocoa, dinosaur blood, and crude oil. Oil— that dirty, greatly loved, money-making stuff was discovered in vast deposits on the north slope of the Brooks Range, and the rush to Alaska began once again.

Big oil companies from around the world made bids for prime locations in hopes of hitting massive gushers of oil. They were correct in their assessments, and it appeared that the North Slope was filled with oil. Then, one of the most controversial issues to hit Alaska began. Transporting those newfound riches from the frozen ground through Alaska to an unfrozen port for transportation to the lower forty-eight had become the biggest problem to be solved.

The natives of Alaska held the rights to much of the land and were strongly opposed to any transportation over their land. The oil companies were willing to pay enormous amounts of money, but still the natives were unwilling to settle. Enough money was finally thrown their way, and a Native Land Claims settlement was secured.

A proposal to build a pipeline from Prudhoe Bay to Valdez eight hundred miles away was the topic of the day for not only Alaskans, but also for Congress.

In 1973, Congress was at a deadlock in the Senate on the construction of the Alaskan Pipeline Authorization Act. Vice President Spiro Agnew cast the deciding vote for the construction to proceed, and the last wilderness came to an end.

The Trans-Alaska pipeline (TAPS) began at Prudhoe Bay in 1973 and was completed in 1977. This pipeline crossed eight hundred rivers and streams, three major mountain ranges, and was buried underground for three hundred eighty miles. It carried 850,000 barrels of crude oil a day and is still functioning today.

The oil companies were thrilled with their pipeline and the prospects of a gas line to follow. The state of Alaska was fat and happy with massive new revenue. The natives' land claims were settled, and even the natives of Alaska were abundantly rich. It seemed everyone was happy with the newfound gold, except the people who lived along the corridor of TAPS and several environmental groups.

This pipeline was to go directly in front of the cabin at Linda Creek, where we had spent the summer mining gold. It ran a quarter of a mile from Earl Boese's cabin and so close to Wiseman, you could walk to it with ease. We were no longer living at Linda Creek, but we still felt the sadness of the destruction of this beautiful and remote area.

A friend who lived along the TAPS corridor was so angered (as were many people living within this area) by this travesty, he took it upon himself to stop, or at least slow down, the development of the pipeline and its destruction of the wilderness. Nightly, he would walk several miles to one of the main construction camps, where he would create as much havoc as he possibly could.

As he walked to the enemy's camp, he would pull survey markers along the route in the hope of causing as much confusion as possible. Arriving at a camp or storage area, he would sabotage their equipment by filling their gas tanks with sugar or water. His mischief was the only way he knew to defend his solitary life of hunting, trapping, and prospecting for gold, and to find peace of mind with the destruction of his perfect life in the remote Brooks Range.

He lost his battle with the pipeline, and it progressed with little thought to the lifestyle of those rugged individuals living in the last wilderness of Alaska. My friend couldn't endure this horrific change to his home. Sadly, he took his own life, and the pipeline continued on its merry way.

With his death reported to the Alaska State Troopers, they arrived to transport his body to Fairbanks. Hub and two other friends built his pinewood casket in our garage. That day, many tears were shed, many beers were drunk, and many colorful stories about his life were told. Then he was flown back home to the Brooks Range, the place he loved the most.

This wasn't the only tragedy created by the pipeline. The small city of Fairbanks turned into a boom town of wild and wooly construction workers from around the world. The prices for everything skyrocketed. Houses that sold for $140,000 in 1973 doubled in price, and rentals were at a premium. One-room shacks without running water were being rented for $500 a month. There was absolutely nowhere for new arrivals to live. Schools were overloaded with the increase of newly-arrived students, and class sizes exploded until more schools were built. Rush hour was a new word to the old-time Alaskans, who never dreamed of having to wait behind other cars, except when a moose was in the road, stopping their passage. Even shopping at the local stores became more difficult and more expensive. Times, they were a-changing, some for the better and some for the worse.

It was a wild new frontier with big oil money luring the local people away from their normal jobs. Teachers, restaurant workers, cab drivers, policemen, and even doctors were being snatched up by one company or another to develop TAPS. With many of the policemen and state troopers joining the pipeline workers, the police force dwindled, and crime became rampant. Prostitutes and pimps were the new color of Fairbanks streets. It was estimated that there were over one hundred fifty prostitutes working the bars and city streets.

Second Avenue of Fairbanks was the local hang-out for the working girls. These girls were so aggressive, even a woman couldn't walk across the street without one of them yelling at you or shaking her bootie for her own entertainment. These newly rich young girls called it 'back gold' and were said to be making more money than the construction workers, and they were undoubtedly having more fun.

Like many of the local people, those big dollar signs turned Hub's head also. He quit his job as a teacher and joined the carpenters/millwrights union to help create this monster pipeline. He worked six weeks at Prudhoe Bay and then returned home for six weeks. This was the standard rotation for many workers, although some had a two-week rotation. Our new lifestyle seemed rather strange to my thinking because we had been one of the few who protested against the building of TAPS. It just goes to show how big money could even entice those who opposed the destruction of Alaska.

With the newfound pipeline money, the lack of adequate schools, and the wild-west attitude of our little town, we sold our home and moved back to the lower forty-eight. Even though Alaska always remains in my heart, I ended up loving my new life as a farmer/rancher in Ellensburg, Washington. It was a lovely place to raise a family, and hunting and fishing were darn good there too.

CHAPTER 17

Alaskan or Inuit Recipes

## Muktuk: the Inuit word for whale blubber

When the first whale of the year is brought into the village, the hunter or the hunter's wife cuts the meat of the fresh whale into pieces to be eaten raw and shared by the entire village. Later, it may be boiled for two or three hours and then preserved in oil. This will be eaten throughout the winter providing generous amounts of vitamin C, a much-needed nutrient for those living in the Arctic. In the past, it was often buried underground and left to age.

## My Muktuk recipe acquired from an elderly Inuit

First you need to marry a good hunter. When he comes home with a whale, you need to be there to welcome him and help cut the whale into big pieces for each person in the village. Cut the outside layer of the whale, and make sure there's some pink layer too. Then hang up what you take home, let it dry for two days. Boil it after it has become a little dry, maybe two hours or more. Put it into a big oil drum, add some seal oil, and you eat it all winter. Then you'll be happy and not get sick.

## Eskimo Ice Cream—akutaq (ah-goo-duck)

This is a delicacy that has kept the Inuits healthy in the Arctic winters for thousands of years. It's always served at special celebrations: potlatches, funerals, weddings, or a young boy's first hunt. It has been carried by hunters on long journeys and credited with their survival.
It seems every village and every family has a favorite recipe, so again I have included my old friend's favorite.

## Akutuq

1 cup caribou fat, finely chopped
1 cup seal oil (whale oil is best)
½ cup water or 2 cups loose snow
Add many handfuls of fresh berries: blueberries, cloudberries, cranberries, salmonberries, or whatever berries you have.

Melt the chopped caribou fat and some oil from the whale in a big pot over a small fire. Then add some oil from the whale and melt it all together. Don't make it too hot. Stir continuously, and add a little water, or better, a cup of snow. Make sure the snow isn't yellow from dog pee. It'll start getting fluffy. Add more snow and whip it. When it's very white, add the berries. Put it outside in the cold, and freeze it. Take it to the party before the kids eat it all.

She also gave me this more modern recipe, but she doesn't make it or like it. She says, "It has no taste and not healthy. A hunter would die, if that's all he had to eat. Not good, but young girls that go to the city make it this way."

## Modern Eskimo Ice Cream

1 cup Crisco
1 cup granulated sugar
½ cup water, berry juice, or 2 cups loose snow (optional)
4 cups fresh berries (blueberries, cloudberries, cranberries, salmon berries, or blackberries)

In a large bowl, cream vegetable shortening and sugar until fluffy. Add water, berry juice, or snow, and beat until fluffy. Fold in berries, and freeze. I'm sure any kids who don't live in the villages wouldn't think this a treat, but Eskimo kids adore it.

## Brooks Range Recipes

**The following recipes were all cooked on a wood-burning stove, so be advised: there will be differences cooking on electric or gas stoves.**

## Dall Sheep Dinner

If you're ever lucky enough to sit down to a dinner of Dall sheep cooked any which way, you're in for a gourmet meal. It doesn't taste like tame sheep or nasty old mutton. It can be the ultimate of wild meat. As any hunter will attest, after you've climbed that high ridge and bagged your sheep, once back in camp, you'll be swiping a piece of meat from the frying pan even before it's fully cooked.
While in the Brooks Range, I think I cooked it every way I could dream up, and it was always delicious. Below was my favorite.

### Seared Dall Sheep Back-strap

The back-strap is the prime cut of all meat and doesn't need any flavor enhancers.

Simply cut into quarter- to half-inch slices, dip in flour, salt, pepper, and over a medium-high heat, brown on both sides in bacon grease. Serve with potatoes and a fresh vegetable.

Chops can be cooked in the same way, or add spices, garlic, tomatoes, your choice

Now you've reached wild game heaven.

### Dall Sheep Roast

It's important to note that fresh meat should be rested for at least one day before eating. This gives the meat time to contract its muscles and adds flavor. It also gives time for any blood to drain. It's just a good idea.

Cut your roasts into any size you desire, but I recommend not too small, because you'll want leftovers. Simply season with salt and pepper, and lay an onion on the top. Place in a 350 oven—judge the cooking time as you would for a beef roast of similar size. This recipe was for a young and tender animal

### Old Dall Sheep Roast

Marinade the roast overnight in soy sauce, a bit of vinegar, some garlic, salt, and pepper.
Wipe the roast dry then add a little bacon grease to a frying pan, and brown on all sides over high heat. Then place in a 275 oven with lots

of onions, some soy sauce, and a cup of water. Cook slowly until tender.

For a really old sheep, I recommend boiling it with lots of spices until tender, then chopping or shredding it into small pieces and serve it over noodles or rice.

## Dall Sheep and Cabbage

Whenever the men went to Wiseman to pick up the mail, Charlie Breck would send me a big cabbage from his garden. Often, we ate it fresh in a coleslaw, but it seemed to go further if I cooked it, and even my baby liked it cooked this way. This is also excellent prepared with caribou or moose.

Dip small pieces of sheep in flour, then salt-and-pepper the heck out of them. Brown sheep in bacon grease. Chop one onion, then braise sheep and onion until golden brown, in a large pot. Add several cups of water, add two bouillon cubes, and maybe a little soy sauce. Cook until meat is tender.
Chop cabbage into desired size. Add cabbage to meat and broth, and cook until cabbage is tender.

## Blueberry Pancakes—my bush recipe

We seldom had eggs, and if we did, they were eaten fried or scrambled, not added to pancakes. This worked rather well without eggs.

1¼ cups flour
1 tbsp baking powder
2 tbsp sugar
1½ cups powdered milk, mixed as directed on packet

A pinch of salt

Add enough blueberries to make you happy. If the batter is too thick, add a little water. Fry on a hot griddle greased with a little cooking oil. Flip over when bubbles start to burst, or when one side looks golden, about two minutes per side

## Linda Creek Bread

*Makes 4 loaves:*
2 packets active dry yeast
4½ cups warm water (110 degrees to 115 degrees)
6 tbsp sugar
2 tbsp salt
¼ cup shortening, melted and cooled
12 cups all-purpose flour, divided

In a large mixing bowl, dissolve yeast in water. Add sugar, salt and shortening; stir until dissolved. Add half the flour; beat until smooth and the batter sheets with a spoon. Mix in enough remaining flour to form a soft dough that cleans the bowl. Turn onto a floured surface. Knead eight to ten minutes or until smooth and elastic. Place in a greased bowl, turning once to grease top. Cover and allow to rise in a warm place until doubled in size: about 1½ hours. Punch dough down. Cover and leave to rise again for 30 minutes.
Divide dough into four parts and shape into loaves. Place in four greased 9 x 5 x 3-inch loaf pans. Cover and leave to rise in a warm place until doubled, about 30-45 minutes. Bake at 375°F for 30-35 minutes or until golden brown. Remove from pans and allow to cool on wire racks.

This bread also makes good cinnamon rolls. Divide dough and using a quarter of the dough, roll it into a rectangle, spread with a little butter, sprinkle with sugar and cinnamon. Roll it like a jelly-roll, and cut into one-inch pieces. Leave to rise and bake. I pour a little maple syrup into the bottom of the baking pan; this makes for some gooey delicious rolls.

### Canned Chicken

Canned chicken might have been the smartest item that Lindy's grocery suggested purchasing by the case. I'm not sure if today they can be found at your local supermarket, but back then it was a popular item. This was a whole boiled chicken submerged in a rich broth and shoved into a can. Like magic, you only needed a can opener, and you had a meal for a special treat or dinner for two or three days. This was as rich and tender as any chicken you would spend hours cooking, but in the bush, it wasn't about the time saved, it was about availability. It was almost impossible to take frozen chicken there and not have it spoil, so this bird-in-a-can was highly appreciated.

I used it for so many things, I would have to write an entire cookbook on the glory of canned chicken. There was no limitation to what you could do with this much-loved old favorite. As much as I cherished it, it would never outdo fresh ptarmigan, but it certainly was quicker and easier than bagging, skinning, cutting, and cooking a wild bird.

### Ptarmigan

The easiest way to dress a ptarmigan is to skin it. I carefully cut the ptarmigan breast meat off the bone or split the breastbone in half. Next, cut the leg and thigh in one piece. Be sure to save the heart, liver, and gizzard for a wonderful soup. A ptarmigan can also be cooked the same as a quail or Cornish game hen, but this is a simple and delicious way to prepare it.

Dredge bird with flour, salt, and pepper. Brown in bacon grease, and then turn the heat to low or simmer. Add a can of beer or a little white wine, and enough water to almost cover the bird. Slowly simmer until tender—maybe 40 minutes to 1 hour.

Option: add a can of mushroom soup, mix with beer or wine. Makes a nice gravy

While living in the bush, beer and wine weren't an option, but I would add a little of Mr. Boese's soy sauce, a bouillon cube, and water. Any bones were re-used for a soup base. Nothing ever went to waste, that was the rule of life in the bush.

## Alaskan Grayling

We were lucky enough to have this lovely fish in the Brooks Range, and I was happy to catch a few. Graylings are rather delicate and best cooked as soon as possible after catching. This is quite a bony fish and difficult to feed to a child because of the amount of small bones. I liked to salt-and-pepper them and throw them on a barbeque, but not having one at Linda Creek, this was my tried-and-true technique:

Cut off the large dorsal fin, tail, and head, then scrape the scales off, and wash fish. Season inside and outside of fish with salt and pepper. Cover bottom of pan generously with bacon grease.
Heat oil till hot, and brown fish quickly on both sides. Enjoy this delicate and delicious fish with a squirt of bottled lemon juice.

## Moose Jerky

This jerky is not very sophisticated, as this is how we made it while camping in the Brooks Range for a month. Hub ate so much, his teeth became loose, but it was about all the meat we had for a couple of weeks.

Cut moose, sheep, or bear into as thin strips as possible. Get your fire smoking with green wood and make a stand of willows over the fire, where it will remain off the heat. Season with salt, pepper, garlic salt—add lots of pepper to keep the flies off. Smoke and dry until it looks good. Eat it then or hang in the sun to complete the drying. It's now ready for your pack or storage

# My Favorite Alaskan Recipes

### Northern Pike

This is how I prepared the record-breaking pike Hub caught in 1972. This served a party of a dozen friends and was fantastic eating. Before barbequing, I filleted the pike down the backbone and then removed the Y bone.
Prepare barbeque. Thinly slice 3-4 onions, and lay them on heavy-duty tinfoil. Lay bacon slices over onions and place fish on the bacon. Season well with salt and pepper. Add more onion slices and another layer of bacon on top of fish. Pour one can of beer over the layers.
Seal tinfoil tightly so that no juices can escape, then place on grill and cover barbeque with lid. After 20 minutes, turn over. Cook for a further 20 minutes.
Move fish to cooler area of fire and check to see if it's cooked. If your fish is smaller, decrease cooking time accordingly.

### Salmon from Seward, Alaska

2 pounds salmon fillets
Garlic powder, salt, pepper
1 cup soy sauce
¼ cup brown sugar
½ cup wine or water

¼ cup vegetable oil

Season salmon with garlic powder, fresh lemon, salt and pepper.
Blend together soy sauce, brown sugar, wine, and vegetable oil until
sugar is dissolved. Place fish in a large resealable plastic bag with
the soy sauce mixture, seal, and turn to coat. Refrigerate for at least 2
hours.
Preheat grill to medium, add smoke-wood chips to fire for a smoky
flavor. Lightly oil grill grate. Place salmon on the preheated grill.
Discard marinade. Cook salmon 6 to 8 minutes per side, or until
cooked to your liking.

### Pickled Salmon

Cut salmon in 4-5 inch pieces, then place in plastic container and
layer with rock salt, fish, rock salt, fish, covering the last fish with
salt. Cover and place in refrigerator overnight.
Rinse fish, and cut into bite-sized pieces, cover in fresh water, and
place in refrigerator for 24 hours.

Prepare pickling solution:

**Pickling Brine**
1 cup sugar, or if you like it sweeter, 1½ cups sugar
3 cups cider vinegar
¾ cup water
A small handful of pickling spices

Simmer for 10 minutes, and cool. Taste the brine, and make
adjustments: it should be quite vinegary. Place salmon and sliced
onions, layering fish, onion, fish in wide mouth jars, and fill with
cooled brine. Close jar with tight fitting lid and refrigerate for 72
hours before eating. This will keep in the refrigerator for several
weeks

## CHAPTER 18
# BUTCHERING AN ANIMAL

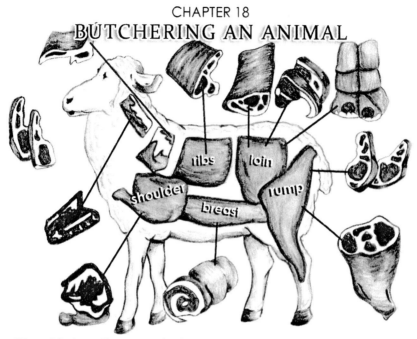

Yes, this is a diagram of a lamb, but can be used for butchering a
Dall sheep, deer, antelope or other small animals.

Hopefully this will be helpful if this is your first butchering
experience.

Items needed:
- Several sharp knives: a boning knife, paring knife, and a
  heavy duty knife
- A whetstone to keep those knives sharp
- Bowl with clean water and several clean rags, or paper
  towels
- Bowl of water with a little vinegar, to wipe meat clean
- Freezer wrap and freezer tape
- Plastic wrap
- Permanent marker

While cutting any meat, after each roast or steak is completed,
scrape off any remaining fat or bone fragments. Wipe the meat clean

with your towel moistened in vinegar, and again wipe dry. This will ensure delicious clean meat ready to be packaged.

I usually begin by cutting the hindquarter off the body completely, making it easier to handle. Next, I cut the round into rolled roasts or steaks, whichever is preferred. I find the bottom round to be a little tough but works well for cubed steak, stew, stir-fry, or slow cooking.

Then you have the yummy sirloin, which I cut into as many steaks as possible. Now you should be down to the shank, and that's where you'll get some hamburger scraps, a huge soup bone and great dog treats. I always debone, meaning I cut all meat away from all the bones. This is just my preference, and it does save room in the freezer. If you prefer your meat cut how it looks in the grocery store, you'll need a good saw and a lot more work.

Next is the rib and loin area, and I seriously don't think I need to recommend anything here. Cut them as big or as small as you want, and invite the neighbors in for a fantastic barbeque. Ribs are the lovely gifts from any animal; other than the fillet, they are tops. In this same area you'll find the loin, and I love the chops from this part of the animal.

Now we're ready for the front shoulder and neck. I remove this from the body, just like removing the hindquarter, making it easier to handle. I think this area has more connective tissue, so trim away to help decide what the choice of cut will be. Some nice chuck steaks or a small roast comes from the upper area. As shown in the diagram, the brisket is towards the bottom and is wonderful cooked slowly at low temperature or brined and smoked. You will again have the shanks to do with what you want, plus the neck.

Please don't forget the tongue, as it's a delicacy not to be forgotten. I boil the tongue until quite tender, then I smoke it. If you don't have a smoker, it's easy to use a barbeque grill, keeping the side where the tongue is turned to off and the other side turned to low. I use mesquite for the smoke, but cherry wood is also great. I use liquid smoke with a little wine for basting and added flavor.

We also cherish the heart and liver, but many people today are skeptical of organ meats. I normally slice the heart and liver thinly and flash-fry. Salt and pepper are the only seasoning I use, but then I fry some onions for a topping.

My biggest recommendation for delicious meat is removing any bloody spots by cutting the area away until it's clean and shows no soft tissue. If left, it will taint the roast or steak, and it just isn't appetizing. I also trim all fat away, as I think that's where you get too much wild taste to your meat.

While cutting the animal, you will have collected little bits and pieces of meat; this is where the burger or stir-fry comes from. If working with a small animal and there aren't enough scraps to grind for burger, just save them for soups or stew.

All the bones can be thrown in the oven and roasted for more flavor or just packaged for later. Wrapping the meat for freezing is an important step too. I first wrap it in plastic wrap, and then freezer paper. It's important to seal each layer tightly, so no air is allowed around your meat. This will assure that your meat isn't ruined by freezer burn after being frozen for a few months.

Bon appétit.

CHAPTER 19
# YOU'RE A SOURDOUGH
## (AN OLD-TIME ALASKAN) IF?

You know a tail-dragger is an airplane, not a bad day at work
.

You think the opening of moose season is a national holiday

You think the four major food groups are: moose, caribou, beer, and salmon

You know salmon isn't a delicacy, it's a staple

You know the words 'haw' and 'gee' mean left and right

You know mush isn't what you eat for breakfast, but a word yelled at your dog team

You refer to the contiguous US as the lower 48

You think the lower 48 is dangerous, and bear hunting is safe

You know how to dance in your bunny boots

You know bunny boots are those huge white boots Alaskans wear in the winter

You think Texas is that smaller state somewhere in the south where they all talk funny

You know what an Arctic entry is, and kick your boots off there before entering a house

You make bets on when the ice will go out on the Nenana River

When someone says they're 'going outside,' you know they mean leaving Alaska

You know if you're driving out of state you need your passport

A traffic jam is ten cars waiting for a moose to cross the road

You know the term 'studs' isn't a hot guy, but winter tires

You think -10 degrees is a bit nippy and +30 degrees is shorts weather

You know 'break-up' isn't about marriage, just the end of winter

You know the phrase 'the kings are running' has nothing to do with royalty, but just another salmon run

Your favorite rhyme is 'Way up north where the huskies go, don't you eat the yellow snow.'

*You are now an honorary Alaskan Sourdough if you actually get these jokes.*

Thank you for reading *The Wild Side of Alaska*, and I hope you enjoyed your Alaskan adventure. I would be honored if you now gave a review, good or bad, on http://www.amazon.com This is the only way writers receive applause, and I would deeply appreciate it.

My other book, *Big Backpack—Little World*, the stories of my teaching ESL around the world for twelve years, is also available on http://www.amazon.com

I can be contacted at:

donnamorang@yahoo.com
esldonna.wordpress.com
http://www.facebook.com/pages/Big-Backpack-Little-World

CPSIA information can be obtained
at www.ICGtesting.com
Printed in the USA
LVOW07s2111120617
537834LV00001B/125/P

9 781490 390833